THIRD EDITION

SUMMIT 2A

ENGLISH FOR TODAY'S WORLD

with WORKBOOK

JOAN SASLOW
ALLEN ASCHER

Summit: English for Today's World Level 3A with Workbook, Third Edition

Pearson, 221 River Street, Hoboken, NJ 07030

Staff credits: The people who made up the *Summit* team representing editorial, production, design, manufacturing, and marketing are Pietro Alongi, Rhea Banker, Peter Benson, Stephanie Bullard, Jennifer Castro, Tracey Munz Cataldo, Rosa Chapinal, Aerin Csigay, Dave Dickey, Gina DiLillo, Christopher Leonowicz, Laurie Neaman, Alison Pei, Sherri Pemberton, Jennifer Raspiller, Mary Rich, Courtney Steers, Katherine Sullivan, and Paula Van Ells.

Cover credit: Tonis Pan/Shutterstock

Text composition: emc design ltd

Library of Congress Cataloging-in-Publication Data

Names: Saslow, Joan M., author. | Ascher, Allen, author.
Title: Summit : English for today's world / Joan Saslow and Allen Ascher.
Description: Third Edition. | White Plains, NY : Pearson Education, [2017]
Identifiers: LCCN 2016017942| ISBN 9780134096070 (book w/ CD) | ISBN 9780134176888 (book w/ CD) | ISBN 013409607X (book w/ CD)
Subjects: LCSH: English language--Textbooks for foreign speakers. | English language--Rhetoric. | English language--Sound recording for foreign speakers.
Classification: LCC PE1128 .S2757 2017 | DDC 428.2/4--dc23
LC record available at https://lccn.loc.gov/2016017942

Student Book

Photo credits: Original photography Mike Cohen. Page 2 Robert Churchill/Alamy Stock Photo; p. 3 (t) Amble Design/Shutterstock, (b) Maximino gomes/Fotolia; p. 4 (l) YUTAKA/AFLO SPORT/Newscom, (r) FRANCISCO TRUJILLO/NOTIMEX/Newscom; p. 5 (r) Alistair Berg/DigitalVision/Getty Images, (l) blvdone/Fotolia; p. 6 (tr) wavebreakmedia/Shutterstock, (b , 1-4) Monkey Business/Shutterstock, DRB Images/LLC/Getty Images, Andersen Ross/Blend Images/Getty Images, Jupiterimages/Stockbyte/Getty Images (b, 5-8) Tracy Whiteside/Shutterstock, Djomas/Shutterstock, Juanmonino/E+/Getty Images, pressmaster/Fotolia; p. 7 YAY Media AS/Alamy Stock Photo; p. 9 (t) Juniart/Shutterstock, (r) Monkey Business/Fotolia, (l) Stefan Schurr/Shutterstock; p. 13 goodluz/Fotolia; p. 15 Andersen Ross/Stockbyte/Getty Images; p. 17 Kzenon/Fotolia; p. 18 petrrunjela/Fotolia; p. 19 Bits and Splits/Fotolia; p. 20 Wavebreak Media Ltd/123RF; p. 21 Zurijeta/Shutterstock; p. 22 (Machal) ROBIN TOWNSEND/EPA/Newscom, (Ka-shing) YONHAP/EPA/Newscom, (Caldicott) Paul Lovelace/REX/Newscom (human rights) tang90246/Fotolia, (smokestacks) Nickolay Khoroshkov/Shutterstock, (refugees) Photo by Antonio Masiello/NurPhoto/REX/Shutterstock, (children in line) Joseph Project - Malawi/Alamy Stock Photo, (school) BSIP/Newscom, (elderly woman and child) Kumar Sriskandan/Alamy Stock Photo; p. 23 demerzel21/Getty Images; p. 26 Drobot Dean/Fotolia; p. 27 ONOKY/Eric Audras/Brand X Pictures/Getty Images, p. 28 (l-r) BMP/Shutterstock, Vladimir Wrangel/Shutterstock, Billion Photos/Shutterstock; p. 29 bertys30/Fotolia; p. 30 (t) Imagewerks/Getty Images, (r) Monkey Business Images/Shutterstock, (l) Racorn/Shutterstock; p. 32 Byron Purvis/AdMedia/Newscom; p. 33 Shariff Che'Lah/123RF; p. 34 Kook Je Newspaper/AP Images; p. 35 (Parks) World History Archive/Alamy Stock Photo, (Khan) Pardis Sabeti, (crocodile) Jeep5d/Fotolia; p. 37 (l-r) Otnaydur/Shutterstock, AVAVA/Fotolia, Andresr/Shutterstock; p. 38 (clockwise) Jade/Blend Images/Getty Images, Andresr/Shutterstock, iofoto/Shutterstock, Monkey Business/Fotolia, nyul/Fotolia, fotogenicstudio/Fotolia, nyul/Fotolia; p. 39 wavebreakmedia/Shutterstock; p. 43 wavebreakmedia/Shutterstock; p. 44 (l) Phil Date/Shutterstock, (r) Jack Hollingsworth/Stockbyte/Getty Images; p. 46 georgerudy/Fotolia; p. 47 gstockstudio/Fotolia, BillionPhotos.com/Fotolia, Mat Hayward/Fotolia, Scott Griessel/Fotolia, Cheryl Savan/Shutterstock, gstockstudio/Fotolia; p. 50 (sand) Douglas Sacha/Moment Open/Getty Images, (caution) jdoms/Fotolia, (bad cat) FotoYakov/Shutterstock, (zipper) memo_frame/Fotolia, (egg) Morrowind/Shutterstock, (corn) Patti McConville/Photographer's Choice/Getty Images, (horse) byllwill/Vetta/Getty Images, (kitten) pavelmayorov/Shutterstock; p. 51 Tom Merton/Hoxton/Getty Images; p. 52 Rouelle Umali Xinhua News Agency/Newscom; p. 53 DragonImages; p. 54 (l) DW labs Incorporated/Shutterstock, (r) east2/Fotolia; p. 55 (laptop/park) wavebreakmedia/Shutterstock, (baby) Cbarnesphotography/E+/Getty Images, (cartoon) Cartoonresource/Shutterstock; p. 57 Tyler Olson/Fotolia.

Illustration credits: Aptara pp. 8, 26, 44, 56; Steve Attoe p. 45; Dusan Petricic pp. 16, 57, 59; el Primo Ramon pp. 10, 14, 31, 58 (t).

Workbook

Photo credits: Page 1 (bottom): Dglimages/Fotolia; 1 (center): Martinan/Fotolia; 1 (top): Blanche/Fotolia; 3: Behyar/Shutterstock; 5 (bottom): Nakophotography/Fotolia; 5 (top): Alysta/Shutterstock; 8: Fantisekhojdysz/Shutterstock; 9: Goodluz/Shutterstock; 16: Ollyy/Shutterstock; 21: Neirfy/Fotolia; 23: Kzenon/Shutterstock; 26 (bottom): Innovatedcaptures/123RF; 26 (center): Joggie Botma/Fotolia; 26 (top): Ikonoklast Fotograÿ e/Shutterstock; 28: Szasz Fabian Jozsef/Fotolia; 29: Rido/Fotolia; 31: Boris Spremo/Toronto Star/Getty Images; 33: Marco Secchi/Getty Images Entertainment/Getty Images; 37: Wong Yu Liang/Fotolia; 38 (bottom): Zhu Difeng/Shutterstock; 38 (bottom, center): Minerva Studio/Fotolia; 38 (top): Gstockstudio/Fotolia; 38 (top, center): Jenner/Fotolia; 40: Mrcats/Fotolia; 41: Yuriy Shevtsov/Fotolia; 43 (bottom): Rocketclips/Fotolia; 43 (bottom, center): Monkey Business/Fotolia; 43 (top): Syda Productions/Fotolia; 43 (top, center): Monkey Business/Fotolia; 45: Brainsil/Fotolia; 48: Fisherss/Shutterstock; 50 (bottom, left): Lek Changply/Shutterstock; 50 (bottom, right): Minerva Studio/Fotolia; 50 (top, left): Ramonespelt/Fotolia; 50 (top, right): Oksana Kuzmina/Fotolia; 51: DPA/The Image Works; 52: OLJ Studio/Shutterstock; 55: Pavelkriuchkov/Fotolia; 56: Everett Collection/Shutterstock.

Illustration Credits: Steve Attoe: pages 4, 56; Stephen Hutchings: page 15; Steve Schulman: page 44; Leanne Franson: pages 14, 17, 20, 53, 57, 58.

Printed in the United States of America

ISBN-10: 0-13-449888-7
ISBN-13: 978-0-13449888-1

6 2020

pearsonelt.com/summit3e

Contents

LEARNING OBJECTIVES

UNIT	COMMUNICATION GOALS	VOCABULARY	GRAMMAR
UNIT 1 **Dreams and Goals** PAGE 2	• Ask about someone's background • Discuss career and study plans • Compare your dreams and goals in life • Describe job qualifications	• Job applications • Collocations for career and study plans • Describing dreams and goals **Word Study:** • Collocations with <u>have</u> and <u>get</u> for qualifications	• Simultaneous and sequential past actions: review and expansion • Completed and uncompleted past actions closely related to the present **GRAMMAR BOOSTER** • Describing past actions and events: review • Stative verbs: non-action and action meanings
UNIT 2 **Character and Responsibility** PAGE 14	• Describe the consequences of lying • Express regret and take responsibility • Explore where values come from • Discuss how best to help others	• Taking or avoiding responsibility • Philanthropic work	• Adjective clauses: review and expansion • "Comment" clauses **GRAMMAR BOOSTER** • Adjective clauses: overview • Grammar for Writing: adjective clauses with quantifiers • Grammar for Writing: reduced adjective clauses
UNIT 3 **Fears, Hardships, and Heroism** PAGE 26	• Express frustration, empathy, and encouragement • Describe how fear affects you physically • Discuss overcoming handicaps and hardships • Examine the nature of heroism	• Expressing frustration, empathy, and encouragement • Physical effects of fear **Word Study:** • Using parts of speech	• Clauses with <u>no matter</u> • Using <u>so</u> … <u>(that)</u> or <u>such</u> … <u>(that)</u> to explain results **GRAMMAR BOOSTER** • Embedded questions: review and common errors • Non-count nouns made countable • Nouns used in both countable and uncountable sense
UNIT 4 **Getting Along with Others** PAGE 38	• Discuss how to overcome shortcomings • Acknowledge inconsiderate behavior • Explain how you handle anger • Explore the qualities of friendship	• Shortcomings • Expressing and controlling anger	• Adverb clauses of condition • Cleft sentences: review and expansion **GRAMMAR BOOSTER** • Grammar for Writing: more conjunctions and transitions • Cleft sentences: more on meaning and use
UNIT 5 **Humor** PAGE 50	• Discuss the health benefits of laughter • Respond to something funny • Analyze what makes us laugh • Explore the limits of humor	• Ways to respond to jokes and other funny things • Common types of jokes • Practical jokes	• Indirect speech: backshifts in tense and time expressions • Questions in indirect speech **GRAMMAR BOOSTER** • Imperatives in indirect speech • Changes to pronouns and possessives • <u>Say</u>, <u>tell</u>, and <u>ask</u> • Other reporting verbs

CONVERSATION STRATEGIES	LISTENING / PRONUNCIATION	READING	WRITING
• Use Thanks for asking to express appreciation for someone's interest. • Use Correct me if I'm wrong, but … to tentatively assert what you believe about someone or something. • Say I've given it some thought and … to introduce a thoughtful opinion. • Informally ask for directions by saying Steer me in the right direction. • Say As a matter of fact to present a relevant fact. • Offer assistance with I'd be more than happy to. • Say I really appreciate it to express gratitude.	**Listening Skills:** • Listen to activate vocabulary • Listen for main ideas • Listen to confirm content • Listen for supporting details • Listen to infer **PRONUNCIATION BOOSTER** • Sentence stress and intonation: review	**Texts:** • An application for employment • An article about two famous people • An article about good and bad interview behavior • A job advertisement • A résumé **Skills / strategies:** • Understand idioms and expressions • Confirm information • Apply ideas	**Task:** • Write a traditional cover letter to an employer **Skill:** • A formal cover letter
• Admit having made a mistake by apologizing with I'm really sorry, but … • Confirm that someone agrees to an offer with if that's OK. • Use That's really not necessary to politely turn down an offer. • Take responsibility for a mistake by saying Please accept my apology.	**Listening Skills:** • Listen to infer information • Listen to support an opinion • Listen for main ideas • Listen to classify • Listen to confirm content • Listen for point of view • Listen to summarize • Listen to draw conclusions **PRONUNCIATION BOOSTER** • Emphatic stress and pitch to express emotion	**Texts:** • A survey about taking or avoiding responsibility • An article about lying • A textbook article about the development of values • Dictionary entries • Short biographies **Skills / strategies:** • Understand idioms and expressions • Relate to personal experience • Classify vocabulary using context • Critical thinking	**Task:** • Write a college application essay **Skill:** • Restrictive and non-restrictive adjective clauses
• Ask Is something wrong? to express concern about someone's state of mind. • Ask What's going on? to show interest in the details of someone's problem. • Begin an explanation with Well, basically to characterize a problem in few words. • Say Hang in there to offer support to someone facing a difficulty. • Say Anytime to acknowledge someone's appreciation and minimize what one has done.	**Listening Skills:** • Listen to predict • Listen to activate parts of speech • Listen for details • Listen to retell a story • Listen to summarize **PRONUNCIATION BOOSTER** • Vowel reduction to /ə/	**Texts:** • A self-test about how fearful you are • Interview responses about how fear affects people physically • An article about Marlee Matlin • Profiles of three heroes **Skills / strategies:** • Understand idioms and expressions • Understand meaning from context • Summarize	**Task:** • Write a short report about a dangerous or frightening event **Skill:** • Reducing adverbial clauses
• Introduce an uncomfortable topic with there's something I need to bring up. • Say I didn't realize that to acknowledge a complaint about your behavior. • Use I didn't mean to … to apologize for and summarize someone's complaint. • Say On the contrary to assure someone that you don't feel the way they think you might. • Say I can see your point to acknowledge someone's point of view.	**Listening Skills:** • Listen to activate grammar • Listen to summarize the main idea • Listen to infer information • Listen to draw conclusions **PRONUNCIATION BOOSTER** • Shifting emphatic stress	**Texts:** • Profiles about people's shortcomings • Descriptions of different workshops • An article on friendship **Skills / strategies:** • Understand idioms and expressions • Understand meaning from context • Apply ideas • Relate to personal experience	**Task:** • Write a three-paragraph essay presenting a solution to a common shortcoming **Skill:** • Transitional topic sentences
• Exclaim You've got to see this! to urge someone to look at something. • Introduce a statement with Seriously to insist someone not hesitate to take your suggestion. • Say That's priceless to strongly praise something. • Agree informally with Totally.	**Listening Skills:** • Listen to activate vocabulary • Listen to summarize • Listen to take notes • Listen to apply ideas **PRONUNCIATION BOOSTER** • Intonation of sarcasm	**Texts:** • A self-test about your sense of humor • An article about the health benefits of laughter • An article about the theories of humor • Descriptions of practical jokes **Skills / strategies:** • Understand idioms and expressions • Critical thinking • Classify	**Task:** • Write a true or imaginary story **Skill:** • Writing dialogue

CONVERSATION STRATEGIES	LISTENING / PRONUNCIATION	READING	WRITING
• Ask a stranger for help with I wonder if you could do me a favor. • Agree to offer assistance with How can I help? • Confirm willingness to perform a favor with I'd be happy to. • Introduce a statement of relief with It's a good thing.	**Listening Skills:** • Listen to infer • Listen to activate grammar • Listen for main ideas • Listen to confirm content • Listen to understand meaning from context • Listen for details • Listen to summarize **PRONUNCIATION BOOSTER** • Regular past participle endings • Reduction in perfect modals	**Texts:** • A travel tips contest • Interview responses about travel hassles • An article about the dangers of public Wi-Fi **Skills / strategies:** • Understand idioms and expressions • Understand meaning from context • Paraphrase • Find supporting details	**Task:** • Write an essay comparing and contrasting two means of transportation **Skill:** • A comparison and contrast essay
• Call someone's attention to an outrageous claim with Can you believe this? • Express surprise at someone's gullibility with Oh, come on. • Use That's got to be to underscore a conclusion. • Add I guess to an opinion one isn't sure about. • Express extreme agreement to another's opinion with You can say that again.	**Listening Skills:** • Listen for details • Listen to confirm content • Listen to summarize • Listen to infer **PRONUNCIATION BOOSTER** • Linking sounds	**Texts:** • A website about superstitions • An article about the placebo and nocebo effects **Skills / strategies:** • Understand idioms and expressions • Infer meaning • Draw conclusions • Critical thinking	**Task:** • Write a four-paragraph essay on superstitions **Skill:** • Subject / verb agreement: expansion
• Say Guess what? to introduce exciting news. • Use I can't make up my mind between … to signal indecision. • Use I wouldn't say … to express modesty or doubt. • Support a statement or point of view with I've been told that. • Provide support for someone's decision with I don't think you can go wrong.	**Listening Skills:** • Listen for main ideas • Listen to infer • Listen for supporting details • Listen to draw conclusions **PRONUNCIATION BOOSTER** • Emphatic stress with auxiliary verbs	**Texts:** • A quiz on emotional intelligence • An article on whether intelligence can be increased • An article on staying on target **Skills / strategies:** • Understand idioms and expressions • Apply ideas • Relate to personal experience	**Task:** • Write a three-paragraph essay about the challenges of staying focused **Skill:** • Explaining cause and result
• Use For one thing to introduce an important first argument. • Say Well, if you ask me … to offer an opinion. • Use I mean to clarify what you just said. • Say I see your point to concede the value of someone else's opinion.	**Listening Skills:** • Listen to activate vocabulary • Listen to identify point of view • Listen to confirm content • Listen to infer information • Listen to draw conclusions **PRONUNCIATION BOOSTER** • Reading aloud	**Texts:** • A survey on future predictions • An article on how people in the past envisioned the future • An article on what some people are doing to protect the environment • Dictionary entries **Skills / strategies:** • Understand idioms and expressions • Understand meaning from context • Draw conclusions	**Task:** • Write a four- or five-paragraph essay about the future **Skill:** • The thesis statement in a formal essay
• Begin a statement with Can you believe … to introduce surprising, exciting, or disturbing information. • Use But on the bright side to change a negative topic to something more positive. • Begin a statement with It just goes to show you … to emphasize a point. • Say Well, that's another story to acknowledge a positive or negative change of topic. • Begin a statement with You'd think … to express frustration with a situation.	**Listening Skills:** • Listen to activate vocabulary • Listen to summarize • Listen to confirm information • Listen to understand meaning from context • Listen to draw conclusions **PRONUNCIATION BOOSTER** • Intonation of tag questions	**Texts:** • A quiz on English in today's world • News stories about global issues and problems • People's opinions about foreign imports • An article about the pros and cons of globalization **Skills / strategies:** • Understand idioms and expressions • Understand meaning from context • Identify supporting ideas • Interpret information in a graph	**Task:** • Write a four-paragraph essay to rebut an opposing view about globalization **Skill:** • Rebutting an opposing point of view

TO THE TEACHER

What is *Summit*?

Summit is a two-level high-intermediate to advanced communicative course that develops confident, culturally fluent English speakers able to navigate the social, travel, and professional situations they will encounter as they use English in their lives. ***Summit*** can follow the intermediate level of any communicative series, including the four-level ***Top Notch*** course.

Summit delivers immediate, demonstrable results in every class session through its proven pedagogy and systematic and intensive recycling of language. Each goal- and achievement-based lesson is tightly correlated to the Can-Do Statements of the Common European Framework of Reference (CEFR). The course is fully benchmarked to the Global Scale of English (GSE).

Each level of ***Summit*** contains material for 60 to 90 hours of classroom instruction. Its full array of additional print and digital components can extend instruction to 120 hours if desired. Furthermore, the entire ***Summit*** course can be tailored to blended learning with its integrated online component, *MyEnglishLab*. ***Summit*** offers more ready-to-use teacher resources than any other course available today.

NEW This third edition represents a major revision of content and has a greatly increased quantity of exercises, both print and digital. Following are some key new features:

- **Conversation Activator Videos** to build communicative competence
- **Discussion Activator Videos** to increase quality and quantity of expression
- A **Test-Taking Skills Booster** (and **Extra Challenge Reading Activities**) to help students succeed in the reading and listening sections of standardized tests
- An **Understand Idioms and Expressions** section in each unit increases the authenticity of student spoken language

Award-Winning Instructional Design*

Demonstrable confirmation of progress
Every two-page lesson has a clearly stated communication goal and culminates in a guided conversation, free discussion, debate, presentation, role play, or project that achieves the goal. Idea framing and notepadding activities lead students to confident spoken expression.

Cultural fluency
Summit audio familiarizes students with a wide variety of native and non-native accents. Discussion activities reflect the topics people of diverse cultural backgrounds talk about in their social and professional lives.

Explicit vocabulary and grammar
Clear captioned illustrations and dictionary-style presentations, all with audio, take the guesswork out of meaning and ensure comprehensible pronunciation. Grammar is embedded in context and presented explicitly for form, meaning, and use. The unique "Recycle this Language" feature encourages active use of newly learned words and grammar during communication practice.

Active listening syllabus
More than 50 listening tasks at each level of ***Summit*** develop critical thinking and crucial listening comprehension skills such as listen for details, main ideas, confirmation of content, inference, and understand meaning from context.

*__*Summit*__ is the recipient of the Association of Educational Publishers' Distinguished Achievement Award.

Conversation and Discussion Activators
Memorable conversation models with audio provide appealing natural social language and conversation strategies essential for post-secondary learners. Rigorous Conversation Activator and Discussion Activator activities with video systematically stimulate recycling of social language, ensuring it is not forgotten. A unique Pronunciation Booster provides lessons and interactive practice, with audio, so students can improve their spoken expression.

Systematic writing skills development
Summit teaches the conventions of correct English writing so students will be prepared for standardized tests, academic study, and professional communication. Lessons cover key writing and rhetorical skills such as using parallel structure and avoiding sentence fragments, run-on sentences, and comma splices. Intensive work in paragraph and essay development ensures confident and successful writing.

Reading skills and strategies
Each unit of ***Summit*** builds critical thinking and key reading skills and strategies such as paraphrasing, drawing conclusions, expressing and supporting an opinion, and activating prior knowledge. Learners develop analytical skills and increase fluency while supporting their answers through speaking.

We wish you and your students enjoyment and success with ***Summit****. We wrote it for you.*
Joan Saslow and Allen Ascher

ActiveTeach

Maximize the impact of your ***Summit*** lessons. Digital Student's Book pages with access to all audio and video provide an interactive classroom experience that can be used with or without an interactive whiteboard (IWB). It includes a full array of easy-to-access digital and printable features.

For class presentation . . .

- **NEW** Conversation Activator videos: increase students' confidence in oral communication
- **NEW** Discussion Activator videos: increase quality and quantity of expression
- **NEW** Extra Grammar Exercises: ensure mastery of grammar
- **NEW** Extra Challenge Reading Activities: help students succeed at standardized proficiency tests.

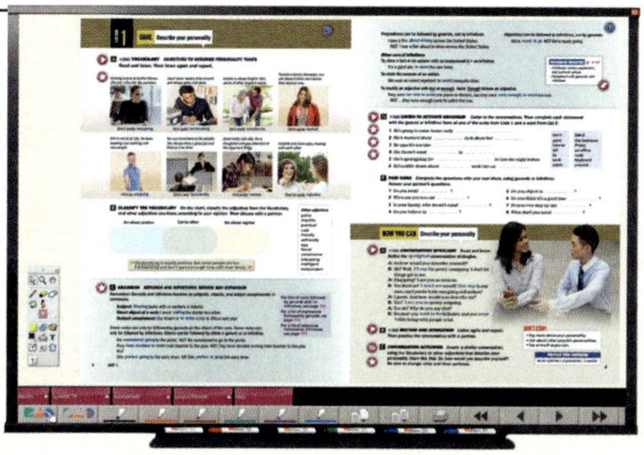

PLUS

- Interactive Whiteboard tools, including zoom, highlight, links, notes, and more.
- Clickable Audio: instant access to the complete classroom audio program
- *Summit TV* Video Program: fully-revised authentic TV documentaries as well as unscripted on-the-street interviews, featuring a variety of regional and non-native accents

For planning . . .

- A *Methods Handbook* for a communicative classroom
- Detailed timed lesson plans for each two-page lesson
- *Summit TV* teaching notes
- Complete answer keys, audio scripts, and video scripts

For extra support . . .

- Hundreds of extra printable activities, with teaching notes
- *Summit TV* activity worksheets

For assessment . . .

- Ready-made unit and review achievement tests with options to edit, add, or delete items.

Ready-made Summit Web Projects provide authentic application of lesson language.

MyEnglishLab

An optional online learning tool

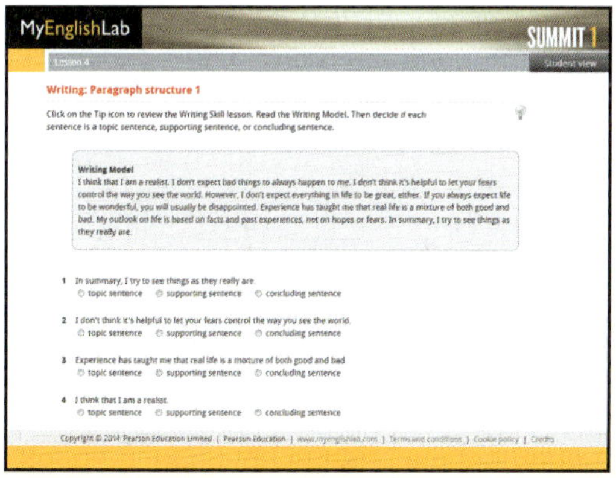

- **NEW** Immediate, meaningful feedback on wrong answers
- **NEW** Remedial grammar exercises
- **NEW** Grammar Coach videos for general reference
- Interactive practice of all material presented in the course
- Grade reports that display performance and time on task
- Auto-graded achievement tests

Workbook

Lesson-by-lesson written exercises to accompany the Student's Book

Full-Course Placement Tests

Choose printable or online version

Classroom Audio Program

- A set of Audio CDs, as an alternative to the clickable audio in ActiveTeach
- Contains a variety of authentic regional and non-native accents to build comprehension of diverse English speakers
- **NEW** The app *Summit Go* allows access anytime, anywhere and lets students practice at their own pace. The entire audio program is also available for students at www.english.com/summit3e.

Teacher's Edition and Lesson Planner

- Detailed interleaved lesson plans, language and culture notes, answer keys, and more
- Also accessible in digital form in ActiveTeach

For more information: www.pearsonelt.com/summit3e

ABOUT THE AUTHORS

Joan Saslow

Joan Saslow has taught in a variety of programs in South America and the United States. She is author or coauthor of a number of widely used courses, some of which are *Ready to Go*, *Workplace Plus*, *Literacy Plus*, and *Top Notch*. She is also author of *English in Context*, a series for reading science and technology. Ms. Saslow was the series director of *True Colors* and *True Voices*. She has participated in the English Language Specialist Program in the U.S. Department of State's Bureau of Educational and Cultural Affairs.

Allen Ascher

Allen Ascher has been a teacher and teacher trainer in China and the United States, as well as academic director of the intensive English program at Hunter College. Mr. Ascher has also been an ELT publisher and was responsible for publication and expansion of numerous well-known courses including *True Colors*, *NorthStar*, the *Longman TOEFL Preparation Series*, and the *Longman Academic Writing Series*. He is coauthor of *Top Notch*, and he wrote the "Teaching Speaking" module of *Teacher Development Interactive*, an online multimedia teacher-training program.

Ms. Saslow and Mr. Ascher are frequent presenters at professional conferences and have been coauthoring courses for teens, adults, and young adults since 2002.

AUTHORS' ACKNOWLEDGMENTS

The authors wish to thank Katherine Klagsbrun for developing the digital Extra Challenge Reading Activities that appear with all reading selections in ***Summit 2***.

The authors are indebted to these reviewers, who provided extensive and detailed feedback and suggestions for ***Summit***, as well as the hundreds of teachers who completed surveys and participated in focus groups.

Cris Asperti, CEL LEP, São Paulo, Brazil • **Diana Alicia Ávila Martínez**, CUEC, Monterrey, Mexico • **Shannon Brown**, Nagoya University of Foreign Studies, Nagoya, Japan • **Cesar Byrd**, Universidad ETAC Campus Chalco, Mexico City, Mexico • **Maria Claudia Campos de Freitas**, Metalanguage, São Paulo, Brazil • **Alvaro Del Castillo Alba**, CBA, Santa Cruz, Bolivia • **Isidro Castro Galván**, Instituto Teocalli, Monterrey, Mexico • **Melisa Celi**, Idiomas Católica, Lima, Peru • **Carlos Celis**, CEL LEP, São Paulo, Brazil • **Jussara Costa e Silva**, Prize Language School, São Paulo, Brazil • **Inara Couto**, CEL LEP, São Paulo, Brazil • **Gemma Crouch**, ICPNA Chiclayo, Peru • **Ingrid Valverde Diaz del Olmo**, ICPNA Cusco, Peru • **Jacqueline Díaz Esquivel**, PROULEX, Guadalajara, Mexico • **María Eid Ceneviva**, CBA, Cochabamba, Bolivia • **Erika Licia Esteves Silva**, Murphy English, São Paulo, Brazil • **Cristian Garay**, Idiomas Católica, Lima, Peru • **Miguel Angel Guerrero Pozos**, PROULEX, Guadalajara, Mexico • **Anderson Francisco Guimarães Maia**, Centro Cultural Brasil Estados Unidos, Belém, Brazil • **Cesar Guzmán**, CAADI Monterrey, Mexico • **César Iván Hernández Escobedo**, PROULEX, Guadalajara, Mexico • **Robert Hinton**, Nihon University, Tokyo, Japan • **Segundo Huanambal Díaz**, ICPNA Chiclayo, Peru • **Chandra Víctor Jacobs Sukahai**, Universidad de Valle de México, Monterrey, Mexico • **Yeni Jiménez Torres**, Centro Colombo Americano Bogotá, Colombia • **Simon Lees**, Nagoya University of Foreign Studies, Nagoya, Japan • **Thomas LeViness**, PROULEX, Guadalajara, Mexico • **Amy Lewis**, Waseda University, Tokyo, Japan • **Luz Libia Rey**, Centro Colombo Americano, Bogotá, Colombia • **Diego López**, Idiomas Católica, Lima, Peru • **Junior Lozano**, Idiomas Católica, Lima, Peru • **Tanja McCandie**, Nanzan University, Nagoya, Japan • **Tammy Martínez Nieves**, Universidad Autónoma de Nuevo León, Monterrey, Mexico • **María Teresa Meléndez Mantilla**, ICPNA Chiclayo, Peru • **Mónica Nomberto**, ICPNA Chiclayo, Peru • **Otilia Ojeda**, Monterrey, Mexico • **Juana Palacios**, Idiomas Católica, Lima, Peru • **Giuseppe Paldino Mayorga**, Jellyfish Learning Center, San Cristobal, Ecuador • **Henry Eduardo Pardo Lamprea**, Universidad Militar Nueva Granada, Colombia • **Dario Paredes**, Centro Colombo Americano, Bogotá, Colombia • **Teresa Noemí Parra Alarcón**, Centro Anglo Americano de Cuernavaca, S.C., Cuernavaca, Mexico • **Carlos Eduardo de la Paz Arroyo**, Centro Anglo Americano de Cuernavaca, S.C., Cuernavaca, Mexico • **José Luis Pérez Treviño**, Instituto Obispado, Monterrey, Mexico • **Evelize Maria Plácido Florian**, São Paulo, Brazil • **Armida Rivas**, Monterrey, Mexico • **Luis Rodríguez Amau**, ICPNA Chiclayo, Peru • **Fabio Ossaamn Rok Kaku**, Prize Language School, São Paulo, Brazil • **Ana María Román Villareal**, CUEC, Monterrey, Mexico • **Reynaldo Romano C.**, CBA, La Paz, Bolivia • **Francisco Rondón**, Centro Colombo Americano, Bogotá, Colombia • **Peter Russell**, Waseda University, Tokyo, Japan • **Rubena St. Louis**, Universidad Simón Bolivar, Caracas, Venezuela • **Marisol Salazar**, Centro Colombo Americano, Bogotá, Colombia • **Miguel Sierra**, Idiomas Católica, Lima, Peru • **Greg Strong**, Aoyama Gakuin University, Tokyo, Japan • **Gerald Talandis**, Toyama University, Toyama, Japan • **Stephen Thompson**, Nagoya University of Foreign Studies, Nagoya, Japan • **José Luis Urbina Hurtado**, Instituto Tecnológico de León, Mexico • **René F. Valdivia Pereyra**, CBA, Santa Cruz, Bolivia • **Magno Alejandro Vivar Hurtado**, Salesian Polytechnic University, Ecuador • **Belkis Yanes**, Caracas, Venezuela • **Holger Zamora**, ICPNA Cusco, Peru • **Maria Cristina Zanon Costa**, Metalanguage, São Paulo, Brazil • **Kathia Zegarra**, Idiomas Católica, Lima, Peru.

UNIT 1

Dreams and Goals

COMMUNICATION GOALS

1 Ask about someone's background
2 Discuss career and study plans
3 Compare your dreams and goals in life
4 Describe job qualifications

PREVIEW

A **FRAME YOUR IDEAS** Complete the first section of an application for employment, using real or invented information.

Application for Employment

PERSONAL INFORMATION

date of application ___ / ___ / ___

Name

last	middle	first

Address	City	State / province	Country	Postal code / zip code

Contact Information

home telephone	cell phone	e-mail

Type of position sought ____________

Available start date ___ / ___ / ___

CURRENT EMPLOYEMENT

Are you currently employed? ☐ yes ☐ no

If so, where? ____________

How long have you worked there? ____________

EDUCATION

	Name	Major field of study	Did you graduate?
High School			
College or University			
Other Education			

SKILLS AND / OR TRAINING: Please list skills and / or training you have had that may contribute to your ability to perform the position you seek:

____

PREVIOUS EMPLOYMENT HISTORY
Please attach a list of previous positions and job responsibilities, starting with the most recent. Include the names and addresses of each company.

STATEMENT OF GOALS
Please attach a short statement about your short-term and long-term employment goals.

To apply online, go to getajob@jobco.com

B ▶ 1:02 **VOCABULARY** **JOB APPLICATIONS** Find and circle these words and phrases in the application. Then listen and repeat.

- employment
- contact information
- position
- start date
- training
- employment history

C **ACTIVATE VOCABULARY** Look at how each word or phrase from Exercise B is used in the job application. Then on a separate sheet of paper, write a definition or synonym for each one.

D **PAIR WORK** What are some do's and don'ts for filling out a job application? With a partner, create a list of suggestions to help an applicant complete a job application successfully.

Be neat and spell all words correctly.

ENGLISH FOR TODAY'S WORLD
Understand a variety of accents.
Anne = Korean
Nina = Spanish

E ▶ 1:03 **SPOTLIGHT** Read and listen to a conversation between two friends discussing career plans. Notice the spotlighted language.

Anne: Well, I finally sent in the applications. Now **it's just wait and see**.
Nina: How many schools did you end up applying to?
Anne: Ten. That's just about every single one within a hundred-mile radius!
Nina: Don't you think **that might be a little overkill**? You shouldn't have any trouble getting in, should you?
Anne: Well, the food industry's so trendy right now, and it's gotten pretty competitive. **I didn't want to take any chances**. This has been a lifelong dream of mine.
Nina: So which one's your first choice? I've read the Taste Institute's pretty good.
Anne: Actually, at first I'd been thinking of going there, but now **I've got my heart set on** the Culinary Center. I've heard it's far superior to the TI.
Nina: The Taste Institute? Really? Aren't chef schools all **six of one, half a dozen of the other**?
Anne: I would have thought so, but it turns out they're not.
Nina: How so?
Anne: Well, the CC's training is more demanding. You've really got to work hard. And their certificate's got a lot more prestige. A CC certificate's a ticket to an interview with all the top restaurants.
Nina: And that's not true with the TI?
Anne: Apparently not. I did a lot of reading, and it seems that the TI's pretty **run-of-the-mill**—nothing wrong with it, but nothing particularly outstanding about it either. **All in all**, the CC's a better bet if I can get in.
Nina: Well, **I'll keep my fingers crossed** for you, Anne. Hope all your dreams come true.

Anne: Thanks! I appreciate that.

F **UNDERSTAND IDIOMS AND EXPRESSIONS** With a partner, paraphrase each of these expressions from Spotlight, saying each one a different way.

1 "… it's just wait and see."
2 "… that might be a little overkill?"
3 "I didn't want to take any chances."
4 "I've got my heart set on … "
5 "… six of one, half a dozen of the other."
6 "run-of-the-mill"
7 "all in all"
8 "I'll keep my fingers crossed … "

G **THINK AND EXPLAIN** Answer the following questions. Explain your answers.

1 Why did Anne apply to so many schools?
2 In your opinion, which of the two reasons Anne gives for preferring the Culinary Center is a better reason? Explain.
3 What does Nina mean when she says, "Hope all your dreams come true"?

SPEAKING Which factors are the most important to you in choosing a job or career? Rate each of the following on a scale of 1 to 5, with 1 being the most important. Then compare charts with a partner, explaining your ratings to each other.

	The training period for the job is short.
	There's not too much competition in the field.
	The work is interesting and fun.
	The pay is good.
	The people in this field are interesting.

	The job has lots of prestige.
	The field is trendy right now.
	The job doesn't require a lot of overtime work.
	The field contributes something important to the world.

LESSON 1

GOAL Ask about someone's background

A ▶ 1:04 **GRAMMAR SPOTLIGHT** Read about two famous people. Notice the spotlighted grammar.

Kohei Uchimura

Kohei Uchimura is considered by some to be the greatest gymnast of all time. He **began** gymnastics very early in life. When Uchimura **joined** Japan's national team at the age of eighteen in 2007, he **had** already **been practicing** gymnastics for fifteen years. And since then, he **has competed** in world-class events year after year and **has won** many prizes and honors. Uchimura trains hard and consistently beats almost all his competition. Although Uchimura **had** already **won** many competitions before the 2012 Olympics, he **had** a close call there and **fell** as he **was dismounting** from the pommel horse. In spite of this, his team **managed** to win the silver medal, so the event **went** into his "win" record anyway. Uchimura has continued to win prize after prize ever since. Uchimura is renowned for the intensity of his concentration during practice. Surprisingly, however, for a world-class athlete, he is known to be pretty relaxed and has a normal life outside of the gym. He's been married since 2012, and he and his wife **had** their first child in 2013.

Singer, songwriter, and actress Lila Downs, whose mother was from Mexico and whose father was from the United States, **grew up** in both countries. She **had learned** to sing as a child and **had performed** with traditional mariachi bands before she **had** any formal training. She **attended** the Institute of Arts in Oaxaca and **studied** classical voice at the University of Minnesota. During the time Downs **was living** in the United States, she **became** more and more interested in the diverse cultural heritage of Mexico. To help support pride in those cultures, Downs **learned** and **incorporated** a variety of indigenous Mexican languages into her songs. One of Downs's other passions is social justice, and the lyrics of some of her songs focus on the stories of workers who **migrated** from rural Mexico to the U.S. Downs has won many prizes, including a Grammy and a Latin Grammy. She and her husband **had been trying** for many years to have a baby, and in 2010, they **adopted** a son. The family travels together on Downs's international singing tours.

Lila Downs

B **DISCUSSION** Is it necessary to have formal training to be an elite athlete or a world-class singer? Support your opinion with reasons and examples.

GRAMMAR BOOSTER p. 128
Describing past actions and events: review

DIGITAL INDUCTIVE ACTIVITY

C **GRAMMAR** **SIMULTANEOUS AND SEQUENTIAL PAST ACTIONS: REVIEW AND EXPANSION**

Review: completed past actions: the simple past tense and the past perfect

The simple past tense describes actions completed in the past, whether or not a specific time is mentioned. Context or time expressions can indicate whether the actions were simultaneous (at the same time) or sequential (one before the other).

When Uchimura **entered** the stadium, the gymnastics event **began**. (= simultaneous completed actions)

Downs **studied** voice in the U.S. **in the years before** she **moved** back to Mexico. (= sequential completed actions)

The simple past tense and the past perfect can be used to describe two sequential completed past actions. However, in informal spoken English it's common to avoid the past perfect and use the simple past tense for both actions, especially when context clarifies the order of occurrence.

Before Uchimura **competed** in the 2012 Olympics, he **had won** several world championships.

> **Remember:** The present perfect can also describe completed past actions.
> Uchimura has competed in world-class events year after year.

Review: simultaneous actions in progress: the past continuous

A statement in the past continuous describes an action that was in progress at a time—or during a period of time—in the past.

Lila Downs **was** already **singing** while I **was looking** for my seat.

> **Remember:** To describe an action that was completed during an action in progress, use the simple past tense.
> Lila met her future husband, Paul, when [or while] she was working in Oaxaca.

Expansion: sequential continuing and completed past actions: the past perfect continuous and the simple past tense

The past perfect continuous can be used to focus on the fact that one past action was already in progress before another one occurred. (It often emphasizes the duration of the action.) Form the past perfect continuous with had been and a present participle. Describe the completed action with the simple past tense.

By the time Downs **moved** to the United States with her parents, she **had been performing** with mariachis for several years.

How long **had** Uchimura **been training** before he **was asked** to join the Japan National Team?

DIGITAL MORE EXERCISES

D ▶ 1:05 **UNDERSTAND THE GRAMMAR** Listen to the conversations and circle the letter of the correct summary of the events. Listen again if necessary.

	a	b
1	**a** They continued filming after he got on the bus.	**b** The bus arrived after the filming was finished.
2	**a** Lisa had been thinking of buying the sweater that she left on the table.	**b** The other girl bought the sweater before Lisa had a chance to try it on.
3	**a** Diane was texting and driving at the same time.	**b** Diane had stopped driving before she texted.

E **GRAMMAR PRACTICE** Complete the statements with the past perfect or past perfect continuous.

1 My brother (had already won / had already been winning) the swim meet when the diving competition began.

2 The house was completely dark when I got home because the family (had gone / had been going) to bed.

3 The audience (had stood / had been standing) in line for hours to buy tickets when they canceled the concert.

4 The women's tennis team (had practiced / had been practicing) on a grass court four times before today's event started.

5 My friend (had already seen / had already been seeing) Lila Downs in concert, so we decided not to go.

NOW YOU CAN Ask about someone's background

A **FRAME YOUR IDEAS** Complete the questionnaire about your background.

Where were you born? ____________ How long have you been living at your current address? ____________

Where had you been living before you moved to your current address? ____________

If you are married, when did you get married? ____________ Where were you living then? ____________

If you have children, what are their names and ages? ____________

If you have a career, what is it? ____________

How long have you been studying English? ____________

If you divided your life into three periods, how would you describe each one?

1. ____________

2. ____________

3. ____________

DIGITAL VIDEO

B **DISCUSSION ACTIVATOR** Get to know a classmate's background. Use the questionnaire as an interview guide. Use the simple past tense, the past perfect, the past continuous, and the past perfect continuous in your questions and answers to clarify events in the past. Say as much as you can.

OPTIONAL WRITING Write a one-page biography of your partner, using the information from your Discussion Activator. Put the biographies together in a notebook or post them on a class blog. Include pictures of the classmates.

Lisa Lee

Lisa has been living in Templeton Towers since February. Before that, she had been living with her family in Easton. She got married in January…

LESSON 2 GOAL Discuss career and study plans

DIGITAL STRATEGIES **A** ▶ 1:06 **VOCABULARY** **COLLOCATIONS FOR CAREER AND STUDY PLANS** Read and listen. Then listen again and repeat.

decide on a course of study or a career
Jonathan decided on a career as a veterinarian because he's interested in medicine and loves animals.

take up something you're interested in
Lida is so impressed by the latest animated films that she's decided to take up computer graphics.

apply for a job or a position in a company
Gary is interested in environmental conservation, so he's applied for a job at the Wildlife Center.

apply to a school or program of study
I hope it's not too late to apply to dental school. I don't want to wait another year.

sign up for a course or an activity
Nora needs math for engineering school, but she hasn't used it since secondary school, so she's signed up for a refresher course.

switch to a new course of study or a career
Magdalena started out in cultural anthropology but soon switched to medicine.

be accepted to / into / by a school or a program
Only two students from our class were accepted to medical school this year.

be rejected by a school or a program
Iris couldn't believe she had been rejected by the Wright College of Music, but luckily she was accepted elsewhere.

enroll in a school or program
Matt has been accepted into flight school, but he won't enroll in the program until next year.

B ▶ 1:07 **LISTEN TO ACTIVATE VOCABULARY** Listen to the conversations. Then listen again. After each conversation, complete the statement with the Vocabulary. Use each collocation only once.

1 She has .... engineering school.
2 She has .... a career in music.
3 He has .... meditation.
4 She has .... two graduate programs.
5 He has .... teaching math.
6 She has .... a position in a medical lab.

C **VOCABULARY PRACTICE** Complete each person's statement, using the Vocabulary. There may be more than one way to answer correctly.

1 I've just .... graduate school!

2 I've been an English teacher all my life, but I've decided to .... teaching French!

3 It may take me years, but my lifelong dream has been to be an architect. I'm going to .... architecture school this year.

4 I retired a few years ago, but I'm bored, so I've just .... law school. My kids think I'm crazy.

5 When I finish school I want to be a conductor, so I've .... the music program at my university.

6 I've just had a baby, but I'm .... an evening program at the college. I want to study graphic design.

7 I want to ride a motorcycle, but my mom and dad won't even let me .... lessons!

8 I'm really a nervous person, but I've .... yoga and it really helps calm me down.

DIGITAL INDUCTIVE ACTIVITY

D GRAMMAR COMPLETED AND UNCOMPLETED PAST ACTIONS CLOSELY RELATED TO THE PRESENT

You can use the present perfect for recently completed actions. The adverbs just, recently, and lately often accompany these statements. (Note: Lately is rarely used in affirmative statements.)

She**'s just been accepted** into a top-notch business school.
Have you **looked** at the program requirements **lately**? They**'ve changed**.

The present perfect continuous can describe an action or event that began in the recent past (and continues in the present and is therefore uncompleted). You can use recently and lately.

We**'ve been filling** out a lot of applications **recently**.

However, the following adverbs are used only with the present perfect, not the present perfect continuous, because they signal a completed action: ever, never, before, already, yet, still (with negative), so far, once, twice, (three) times.

Have you **ever** considered applying to graduate school? I **never** have.
I **still** haven't signed up for lifeguard training.

Be careful!
Use the simple past tense, not the present perfect, to talk about actions completed at a specific time in the past.
She applied for a position at the Science Institute last week.
NOT She ~~has applied~~ for the position at the Science Institute last week.

Remember: Don't use the present perfect continuous with these stative verbs: be, believe, hate, have (for possession), know, like, love, own, seem, understand.
DON'T SAY I~~'ve been knowing~~ him for a year.

GRAMMAR BOOSTER p. 128
Stative verbs: non-action and action meanings

DIGITAL MORE EXERCISES

E GRAMMAR PRACTICE Circle the correct verb phrase to complete each statement.

1 In 2016, I (have enrolled in / enrolled in) the computer graphics program.
2 I still (haven't been receiving / haven't received) an acceptance letter.
3 No one (saw / has seen) Mike lately.
4 We (haven't been signing up / haven't signed up) for the professional development course yet.
5 The class (has started / started) at 9:00 sharp.
6 Lately, she's (been getting / got) ready to apply for that new position.

F GRAMMAR PRACTICE On a separate sheet of paper, write five questions to ask someone about his or her career or education plans. Use the present perfect, the simple past tense, and appropriate adverbs.

PRONUNCIATION BOOSTER p. 143
Sentence stress and intonation: review

NOW YOU CAN Discuss career and study plans

A ▶1:08 CONVERSATION SPOTLIGHT Read and listen. Notice the spotlighted conversation strategies.

A: So, Vanessa, have you decided on a career yet?
B: **Thanks for asking**. Actually, I've been thinking of taking up social work.
A: Social work. That's interesting. **Correct me if I'm wrong, but** weren't you a biology major?
B: Yes, that's right. But **I've given it some thought and** decided science just isn't for me.
A: So how can I help?
B: Well, I'd like to enroll in a good graduate program. I was hoping you could **steer me in the right direction**.
A: **As a matter of fact** we have a great program right here. **I'd be more than happy to** write you a recommendation.
B: That's super! **I really appreciate it**.

B ▶1:09 RHYTHM AND INTONATION Listen again and repeat. Then practice the conversation with a partner.

DIGITAL VIDEO
DIGITAL SPEAKING BOOSTER

C CONVERSATION ACTIVATOR Create a similar conversation, using the questions you wrote in Exercise F. Start like this: *So, have you decided on ...* Be sure to change roles and then partners.

DON'T STOP!
- Discuss your background and interests.
- Say as much as you can.

LESSON 3 **GOAL** Compare your dreams and goals in life

A ▶ 1:10 **LISTENING WARM-UP VOCABULARY DESCRIBING DREAMS AND GOALS** Read and listen to what the people are saying. Then listen again and repeat the verb phrases and adjectives.

DIGITAL STRATEGIES

I'm fulfilling my lifelong dream to be an archaeologist. I'm in a graduate program and expect to get my degree in three years.

I know the goal I've set is ambitious, but I don't think it's unrealistic.

My husband will be working from home for the next three years so we can share the housekeeping and childcare responsibilities 50-50.

Verb phrases
- fulfill a dream
- set a goal
- work towards / pursue a goal
- put [something] off
- share responsibilities

Adjectives	
ambitious	modest
achievable	unachievable
realistic	unrealistic

My wife put off her studies and worked to support us while I was studying. Now it's my turn to support her as she pursues her goal.

If we have a common goal and work towards it, anything's achievable. Hey, the sky's the limit for us!

B **ACTIVATE THE VOCABULARY** Complete each statement, using a word or phrase from the Vocabulary.

1 One way a husband and wife can .... is by each one doing half of the household chores.

2 Sometimes a goal requires too much work and it becomes ....

3 When you finally achieve what you've wanted all your life, you have ....

4 .... is an adjective that means almost the same thing as "challenging."

5 Sometimes people .... working towards their own goals for a while in order to help a spouse pursue his or her own goals for now.

6 The first step in achieving something is to ....

DIGITAL STRATEGIES

C ▶ 1:11 **LISTEN FOR MAIN IDEAS** Listen. Complete each statement, choosing the correct word or phrase.

1 Dan stays home because he (lost his job / wants to stay home).

2 Sarah is the primary (breadwinner / caregiver) in the family.

3 Sarah's lifelong dream was to be (a stay-at-home mom / a surgeon).

4 The number of (mothers / fathers) who choose to stay home to take care of the children is increasing.

5 Dan and Sarah have decided to lead a (traditional / nontraditional) lifestyle.

D ▶ 1:12 **LISTEN TO CONFIRM CONTENT** Write a checkmark next to the topics that were discussed. Write an X next to the topics that weren't. Listen again to check your answers.

- ☐ the definition of a stay-at-home dad
- ☐ the number of stay-at-home dads in the U.S.
- ☐ the kind of work Dan did before the children were born
- ☐ the ages of Dan and Sarah's children
- ☐ the sexes of Dan and Sarah's children
- ☐ the number of years it took for Sarah to complete her degree

E LISTEN FOR SUPPORTING DETAILS On a separate sheet of paper, answer each question. Explain your answers with details from what Dan said. Listen again if necessary.

> "He's happy because he's doing what he always wanted to do."

1 Is Dan happy with his lifestyle choice? How do you know?
2 Why does Dan think comments about his life choices are sexist?
3 What's Dan's opinion of women who become the primary breadwinner of the family?
4 Why does Dan think it's good for his children to observe the roles he and Sarah have taken?
5 Why would the person who sent the tweet be against his son's deciding to be a stay-at-home dad?
6 How do you know Dan doesn't like the terms *housewife* and *househusband*?
7 What's Dan's hope for the next generation?

F DISCUSSION Discuss the following questions. Express and support your opinions.

1 Should any careers or parental / household roles be limited to people of one sex or the other? Be specific and support your opinion with reasons.
2 Why do people have a double standard for men and women? Is there any good reason to have one?
3 Will Dan and Sarah's children benefit or be harmed by their parents' reversal of roles. In what ways?
4 Are men or women naturally more ambitious in their careers? If you think they are, why do you think that is?
5 Do you think Dan and Sarah fulfilled their dreams and goals? If so, explain how.

NOW YOU CAN Compare your dreams and goals in life

A FRAME YOUR IDEAS Complete the chart with your own dreams and goals. If you need more space, continue on a separate sheet of paper.

Goals I've set	What I have done to achieve them
to get married and have three children	*I've signed up for an online dating site.*

	Goals I've set	What I have done to achieve them
for my family		
for my career		
other		

RECYCLE THIS LANGUAGE

- decide on
- take up
- apply for / to
- sign up for
- switch to
- be accepted to / into / by
- be rejected by
- a breadwinner
- a caregiver
- sexist
- traditional
- have a double standard

DIGITAL SPEAKING BOOSTER

B DISCUSSION Share and compare goals with your partner. Use the Vocabulary from page 8.

LESSON 4 **GOAL** Describe job qualifications

A READING WARM-UP How qualified are you for the job you want—now or in the future? Explain.

DIGITAL STRATEGIES **B** ▶ 1:13 **READING** Read the article about good and bad interview behavior. In your opinion, which suggestion is the most important?

JOB BUILDER

Home | About | Advice & tips | Build a career | Search

The Successful Job Interview

Charlotte Watson

OK. So you've sent in an application and a résumé for that dream job you saw advertised. The employer thinks you might be a good candidate, and you've landed an interview. You already know it's important to dress right, offer a firm handshake, and maintain eye contact, but do you know that other aspects of your behavior can make the difference between getting that job or not?

Being late to a job interview is almost always a disqualifier. Most candidates are on their best behavior for their interview, so being late is a major red flag for employers. Since punctuality is expected in any kind of work setting, arriving late makes your future employer think you'll be late for work if you get the job. If you are late for your interview, it's important to provide an airtight detailed excuse, explaining why your lateness was unavoidable. Apologize and reassure the interviewer that this isn't habitual behavior on your part.

Another thing that can get an interviewee off on the wrong foot is being overly informal or too familiar. Even though the person who interviews you might be friendly or dressed informally, don't take this as permission to be inappropriately casual. If an interviewer wants to be addressed by his or her first name, he or she will invite you to do that. If not, be sure to stick with last names and titles.

Remember that employers want to know that you are interested in the job and will be a motivated employee. A candidate who hasn't taken the time to learn something about the company or the position being offered appears unmotivated and willing to take anything that comes along. Even if you are sure you already know everything you need to know about the job or the company, prepare two or three relevant questions for the interviewer of the position. And listen with obvious interest to the answers, following up with thoughtful questions that demonstrate that you have been listening.

So before your next job interview, check out the list of do's and don'ts and follow the suggestions. They'll take you a long way towards getting that dream job!

Top Ten Do's and Don'ts for Your Job Interview

Do	Don't
Arrive on time.	Be too familiar.
Stay on topic when answering questions.	Talk too much.
Ask questions.	Seem desperate to get the job.
Listen.	Criticize your current employer.
Be modest, yet positive about yourself.	Brag about yourself.

C CONFIRM INFORMATION Write a checkmark for the ideas that Charlotte Watson expressed in the article. Then, for the statements that don't reflect what she said, work with a partner to clarify what she did say.

☐ **1** Employers expect employees to be punctual on the job.

☐ **2** You shouldn't ask the employer questions during a job interview because it might indicate that you don't know anything about the company.

☐ **3** It's important for job candidates to express interest in the company offering the job.

☐ **4** Employers should dress informally when they interview job candidates.

☐ **5** It's better not to explain why you are late for an interview.

D APPLY IDEAS Read more things Ms. Bates said in her interview. With a partner, explain whether she followed Watson's suggestions.

1 "I'd say I'm kind of a people person and a pretty good listener. My colleagues often come to me when they need advice and support."

2 "Correct me if I'm wrong, Ian—you're married, right?"

3 "I really can't stand my supervisor. He's not fair. If I don't get this job, I'll be very depressed!"

4 "I make even better presentations than my boss. You would be lucky to have me in this job."

5 "What is the biggest challenge the company sees itself facing in the next year?"

6 "Let me tell you what my teacher did when I was still a child. My mother was visiting and the teacher showed her my artwork, which she said was the best in the class. And since this job entails creating presentations at meetings, I thought that information would indicate that this has been a lifelong interest of mine and something that I have developed a lot of skills in."

DIGITAL EXTRA CHALLENGE

E DISCUSSION Explain the reason for each of the do's and dont's on the list in the article.

"If you criticize your current employer, the interviewer could think you're not a loyal employee and might say bad things about his or her company too."

DIGITAL STRATEGIES

F ▶ 1:14 **WORD STUDY COLLOCATIONS WITH HAVE AND GET FOR QUALIFICATIONS**
Read and listen to the collocations, paying attention to have, get, and the prepositions. Repeat.

have experience	**get experience in**
have experience with	**get training in**
have experience in	**get a degree / certificate in**
have training in	**get certified in**

G PERSONALIZE THE VOCABULARY On a separate sheet of paper, write statements about your qualifications, using at least four of the collocations.

I've had some training in IT and gotten some experience in managing technical staff ...

NOW YOU CAN Describe job qualifications

A FRAME YOUR IDEAS Read the job ad and Ben Breeden's résumé. With a partner, make notes describing his qualifications for this job. Use the collocations from Word Study.

Wilton Hotel, Miami FLORIDA, USA

Seeks Assistant Manager to work at front desk and in office. Must possess good people skills and knowledge of the hotel industry. The Wilton Hotel has many guests and workers from Latin America so ability to speak Spanish and Portuguese fluently a must.

Ben Breeden

102 Shanley Avenue
Newtown, FL 32793

+1 555 776 9833
ben.breeden@blue.net

Objective
To use my background and experience in a managerial position in the hotel industry

Experience
July 2016 to the present
Corporate sales associate, Holiday House Hotel, Newtown, FL

August 2015 to June 2016
Event planning assistant, Holiday House Hotel, Newtown, FL

September 2013 to June 2015
Part-time salesclerk, Pennyworth's Department Store, Newtown, FL

Education
Comstock School of Hotel Management, Comstock, GA
Certificate in Hotel Management (June 2015)

University of Central Florida, Hyperion, FL
B.S. in Communication with major in Spanish and Portuguese (June 2014)

B ROLE PLAY In pairs, role-play a job interview between Ben Breeden and the hiring manager of the Wilton Hotel. Follow Charlotte Watson's suggestions.

OPTIONAL WRITING Write your own one-page résumé. Include your employment history, education and / or training. Use Breeden's résumé as a model, or select a template from an online résumé-building website.

WRITING A formal cover letter

A **WRITING SKILL** Study the rules.

The purpose of a cover letter is to acquaint an employer with you and to express interest in a position. If a job ad provides instructions about what to include in your cover letter, be sure to follow the directions carefully. If you don't, you may not receive a response. The letter can be sent in traditional paper form by mail, or as an e-mail.

Traditional paper form

Follow the style used for other formal letters. Use good quality paper and be neat. Proofread your letter carefully to be sure there are no spelling mistakes or typographical errors. Try to limit the letter to one page. Include your résumé on a separate sheet of paper in the same envelope.

E-mail form

Use formal e-mail style, addressing the recipient with his or her title and last name followed by a colon. Make paragraphs easy to read by separating them with a blank line space. Do not attach your cover letter to your e-mail. Make the e-mail the actual cover letter so the recipient can see the information upon opening the e-mail. Attach your résumé to your e-mail.

Here are some suggestions:

- Tell the employer why you are writing (in response to an ad, as a general expression of interest in working at that company or institution, etc.).
- Say why you think you would be a good candidate for the (or a) position; i.e., briefly state your qualifications.
- Tell the employer how to contact you for follow-up or to schedule an interview.
- Do not include too much information about your life.

WRITING MODEL

Celina Ingram
95 River Road
Newtown, FL 32791
+1 555 887 7930
celina.ingram@blue.net — your address

October 2, 2018 — date

Mr. Ian Howe
Human Resources
Clermont Greeting Cards
7200 Bay Blvd
Seattle, WA 32555 — recipient's address

Dear Mr. Howe, — salutation

I am writing in response to your advertisement on giantjob.com for the executive administrative assistant position at the Clermont Card Company in Seattle.

I have often bought Clermont greeting cards because of their positive messages and nice graphics, which is why I would be proud to work there. In addition, I believe I would be a good candidate because of my successful experience as an administrative assistant at Pinkerton Greeting Cards.

I have attached my résumé and the names and contact information of two managers here at Pinkerton who have offered to provide a recommendation.

If you agree that my experience and other qualifications make me a good candidate, please contact me at the address or e-mail address above. As I will be moving to Seattle in two weeks, please contact me at my e-mail address after October 15.

I look forward to hearing from you.

Cordially, — complimentary close

Celina Ingram — signature

Celina Ingram — typewritten name

attachment — indicates another document included in the same envelope

B **PRACTICE** Read the e-mail cover letter. On a separate sheet of paper, rewrite it, correcting errors in style and formality.

Subject:

Hi, Bill—Just wanted u 2 know Im intersted in that great advertising copy writer job I saw listed in the want ads ☺. I think I'm the rite person 4 u. Here's why: I am 26 years old and graduated from Meecham College with a major in english. I have been working at Poco Cola in the advertising department for five years I am ready to move to a new company. My résumé is attached so you can see my qualifications. If you are interested in discussing the job, please e-mail me at the address above to set up an interview. -Jon

DIGITAL WRITING PROCESS

C **APPLY THE WRITING SKILL** On a separate sheet of paper, write a formal cover letter to an employer, expressing interest in a job. Create a job title that interests you and use the name of a real or a fictitious employer. Use real or invented information.

SELF-CHECK

- ☐ Does my letter have any spelling, punctuation, or typographical errors?
- ☐ Did I use formal letter writing conventions?
- ☐ Did I tell the employer the purpose of my letter?
- ☐ Did I say why I think I would be a good candidate?
- ☐ Did I tell the employer how to contact me for follow-up?

DIGITAL GAME

REVIEW

A ▶ 1:15 **Listen to the conversations. Then read the questions in the chart and listen again. Complete the chart after each conversation.**

	What is his or her dream in life?	Is he or she confident about achieving his or her goal?	
1		☐ yes	☐ no
2		☐ yes	☐ no
3		☐ yes	☐ no
4		☐ yes	☐ no

B Complete the statements with the correct prepositions.

1 She has always wanted to take .... the piano and has enrolled .... a program that teaches the basics of music to adults.

2 Anyone applying .... a job in the newspaper business should have training .... journalism.

3 He has decided .... a career as a chef and has been accepted .... a top-notch cooking school in Peru.

4 Her experience .... the diplomatic service and her degree .... international relations make her an excellent candidate for a position at the U.N.

5 After being rejected .... two accounting firms for a summer internship, he decided to switch .... a different major at his university.

6 Before she applied .... law school, she signed up .... speed reading.

C Match each word or phrase with its definition. Then, on a separate sheet of paper, use each one in a statement about your own plans and goals.

...... **1** achievable — **a** capable of being reached

...... **2** ambitious — **b** decide what one wants to do and work towards it

...... **3** work towards a goal — **c** divide necessary work between two or more people so neither one has to do it all

...... **4** put off — **d** postpone

...... **5** unrealistic — **e** requiring a lot of work

...... **6** share responsibilities — **f** unreasonably hard and thus unlikely to be achieved

D Complete each information question, using the past perfect continuous.

1 (how long / you / work on) .... that project before you changed jobs?

2 (where / they / study) .... before they moved to Europe?

3 (which program / she / apply for) .... when she decided to change majors?

4 (what professor / you / study with) .... when they closed the university?

5 (how long / they / look) .... at résumés before they saw yours?

TEST-TAKING SKILLS BOOSTER p. 151

Web Project: Careers
www.english.com/summit3e

UNIT

2 Character and Responsibility

COMMUNICATION GOALS

1 Describe the consequences of lying
2 Express regret and take responsibility
3 Explore where values come from
4 Discuss how best to help others

PREVIEW

A FRAME YOUR IDEAS Look at the pictures. Then answer the questions in the survey. Check what you would do in each situation.

Taking responsibility... or avoiding it

IS IT HARD FOR YOU TO ACCEPT RESPONSIBILITY?

What would you do if you ...	A	B	C	Other
☐ made a serious mistake at work or school?	☐	☐	☐	☐
☐ forgot to finish an assignment at work or school?	☐	☐	☐	☐
☐ broke or lost something you had borrowed?	☐	☐	☐	☐
☐ were late for an appointment?	☐	☐	☐	☐
☐ were stopped for exceeding the speed limit?	☐	☐	☐	☐
☐ damaged someone's car while parking, but no one saw you?	☐	☐	☐	☐
☐ hadn't kept a promise you made to a friend or relative?	☐	☐	☐	☐
☐ forgot a friend's birthday?	☐	☐	☐	☐
☐ were caught telling a lie?	☐	☐	☐	☐

A I would admit making a mistake.

B I would shift the blame to someone or something else.

C I would make up an excuse.

B ▶ 1:16 **VOCABULARY TAKING OR AVOIDING RESPONSIBILITY** Listen and repeat.

- admit making a mistake
- make up an excuse
- shift the blame
- keep a promise
- tell a lie / tell the truth

C PAIR WORK Compare and explain your responses to the survey.

D DISCUSSION Are there ever good reasons *not* to be truthful? Is it ever a better idea to make up an excuse or shift the blame to someone else? Explain your answers and give examples.

ENGLISH FOR TODAY'S WORLD
Understand a variety accents.
Jason = American English (regional)
Dad = American English (regional)

E ▶ 1:17 **SPOTLIGHT** Read and listen to a conversation between a father and his teenage son. Notice the spotlighted language.

Jason: Dad … I think I messed up big time today.
Dad: What happened?
Jason: Well, you know how teachers always like to put up students' artwork on the walls? So Joey and I noticed this really weird drawing of a horse.
Dad: So what? You didn't like it. That's not a crime.
Jason: True. But that's not all.
Dad: Uh-oh.
Jason: See, Mr. Rogg had to step out for a bit. And Joey—you know how he's always fooling around—he starts **making fun of** the drawing, acting like he's the horse.
Dad: And I suppose the class loved that?
Jason: Totally. Everyone was cracking up. Anyway, I **couldn't help myself**. I started joking around, too, and I guess we just kind of **got carried away**.
Dad: Don't tell me the kid who drew it was in that class!
Jason: No one realized it until she got up and ran out.
Dad: Wow. Her feelings must have really been hurt.
Jason: **That's not the worst of it**. She came back with Mr. Rogg and she was crying, which made me feel awful. I could just kick myself! I wish I'd told Joey to **cut it out**.
Dad: Well, it's never too late to apologize. If I were you, I'd **own up to** what you did and tell her how bad you feel. Take responsibility for **letting things get out of hand**. Maybe later you could **make it up to her** by buying her lunch.
Jason: You're probably right.
Dad: And it wouldn't hurt to talk to Mr. Rogg afterward … just so he knows you did the right thing.

F **UNDERSTANDING IDIOMS AND EXPRESSIONS 1** Find two spotlighted expressions that mean someone allowed his or her behavior to go too far.

G **UNDERSTANDING IDIOMS AND EXPRESSIONS 2** Complete the statements.

1 "Making fun of something" means …… .
2 "Couldn't help myself" means …… .
3 "That's not the worst of it" means …… .
4 "Cut it out" means …… .
5 "Own up to something" means …… .
6 "Make it up to someone" means …… .

a admit you did it and take responsibility for it.
b "Stop doing that!"
c do something nice for someone you have wronged.
d joking about it in order to criticize it.
e wasn't able to stop doing [something].
f there's even more negative information.

H **DISCUSSION** Discuss the questions.

1 Whose responsibility was it to prevent what happened in the art class—Joey's, Jason's, Mr. Rogg's, or the girl's? Explain.
2 In what way could Joey, Jason, Mr. Rogg, or the girl have handled the situation differently?

SPEAKING **PAIR WORK** Tell a partner about a situation in which someone's feelings were accidentally hurt. How was the situation resolved? Use the Vocabulary from page 14 and expressions from Spotlight.

LESSON 1 **GOAL** Describe the consequences of lying

A ▶ 1:18 **GRAMMAR SPOTLIGHT** Read the article. Notice the spotlighted grammar.

"Telling the Truth? It's Not So Easy!"

The honest truth? We *all* tell lies. In a psychological study, 147 participants were asked to keep a diary of the lies they told over the course of a week. Researchers found that:

- Participants told lies to about 30 percent of the people **with whom they interacted**.
- There wasn't a single day **when the participants didn't tell at least one lie**.

In fact, we live in a world **where we are often punished for telling the truth and rewarded for lying**. For example, we tell our boss we got stuck in traffic instead of admitting that we overslept. Making up an excuse keeps us out of trouble.

Here's another common situation **in which we often tell lies**: we pretend to like something to avoid hurting others. For example, we say we love a friend's gift when in fact we don't like it.

Some researchers argue that lying may in fact be good for us socially because it protects the feelings of the people **with whom we interact**. Interestingly, they note that the people **whose professions require the most social contacts**—for example, store clerks, salespeople, politicians, and journalists—tell the most lies.

The truth is, everyone tells "white lies" to avoid hurting others. Sometime **when you're ready**, try keeping a diary for a week and see how long you can go without telling a single lie!

B **APPLY IDEAS** With a partner, brainstorm one or more additional situations in which people would be likely to tell a lie, according to the article. Explain why.

C **EXPRESS AND SUPPORT AN OPINION** Do you agree that "lying may in fact be good for us socially because it protects the feelings of the people with whom we interact"? Explain, using examples from your life if possible.

D **PAIR WORK** How truthful are you? Write an X on the continuum. Explain your choice to your partner, giving examples from your experience.

NEVER TRUTHFUL ⟵ SOMETIMES TRUTHFUL ⟶ ALWAYS TRUTHFUL

E **RELATE TO PERSONAL EXPERIENCE** Discuss and then make a list of times in your life when you ...

- made an excuse to avoid getting in trouble.
- told a lie to avoid hurting someone else's feelings.
- were punished or got in trouble after telling the truth.
- were rewarded for telling a lie.

GRAMMAR BOOSTER p. 129
- Adjective clauses: overview
- Adjective clauses with quantifiers

DIGITAL INDUCTIVE ACTIVITY

F **GRAMMAR ADJECTIVE CLAUSES: REVIEW AND EXPANSION**

Remember: An adjective clause gives more information about a noun. The relative pronouns who, whom, and that introduce adjective clauses about people. The relative pronouns that and which introduce adjective clauses about things.

The participants **who kept a diary** recorded that they told lies every day. (who = the participants)
White lies are some of the most common lies **that people tell**. (that = the most common lies)

Use when, where, and whose to introduce adjective clauses about time, location, and possession.

Time: There has never been a time **when** some form of lying wasn't a part of everyday life.
Location: There's no place in the world **where** people are completely honest all the time.
Possession: People **whose** jobs require frequent social contact have the most opportunity to lie.

In formal English, when a relative pronoun is the object of a preposition, the preposition appears at the beginning of the clause. In informal English, the preposition usually appears at the end.

The participants lied to many of the people **with whom** they interacted. (formal)
The participants lied to many of the people **who** they interacted **with**. (informal)

It's a question **to which** most people don't give a truthful answer. (formal)
It's a question **which** most people don't give a truthful answer **to**. (informal)

Be careful!
Use whom, not who, directly after a preposition.
... **with whom** they interacted.
NOT ~~with who~~ they interacted.
Use which, not that, directly after a preposition.
... **to which** most people don't give a truthful answer.
NOT ~~to that~~ most people don't give a truthful answer.

DIGITAL MORE EXERCISES

G UNDERSTAND THE GRAMMAR With a partner, study the adjective clauses in Grammar Spotlight on page 16 and answer the questions.

1 Which adjective clause is about possession? Which is about location? Which are about time?
2 Which three are objects of a preposition? On a separate sheet of paper, rewrite those sentences in informal English.

H GRAMMAR PRACTICE Complete the sentences with one of the relative pronouns from the box. (Do not add any prepositions.)

who	whom
which	whose
where	when

1 The workplace is the place .... people tend to tell the most lies.
2 People .... lies are discovered lose the trust of their friends and colleagues.
3 The people with .... I work are trustworthy.
4 People .... break their promises cannot be trusted.
5 There are situations in .... it's impossible to tell the truth.
6 There are moments .... being honest can cause you problems.
7 The people to .... I never lie are the people .... are really close to me.
8 There are times .... I lie to avoid getting into trouble and times .... I lie to avoid hurting others.
9 Telling the truth is an action for .... there is sometimes no reward.
10 The people .... lies were recorded said they would tell about 75 percent of those lies again.

NOW YOU CAN Describe the consequences of lying

A NOTEPADDING With a partner, write examples for each category.

Situations in which we shouldn't tell lies	Situations in which telling a lie is the best solution

B ACTIVATE THE GRAMMAR On a separate sheet of paper, describe the consequences of lying in the situations on your notepad. Use adjective clauses.

Lying to someone who is a good friend is wrong.
You could destroy the friendship that way.

DIGITAL VIDEO

C DISCUSSION ACTIVATOR Discuss the consequences of lying. Explain further by providing examples. Say as much as you can.

LESSON 2

GOAL Express regret and take responsibility

A ▶ 1:19 **LISTEN TO INFER INFORMATION** Listen to the conversations. Then listen again and choose the expression that best describes each person's behavior.

1 She ...... the damage.
  a took responsibility for b avoided taking responsibility for
2 He ...... the damage.
  a took responsibility for b avoided taking responsibility for
3 He ....
  a admitted making a mistake b shifted the blame to someone else
4 She ....
  a admitted making a mistake b made up an excuse
5 She ...... for being late.
  a took responsibility b made up an excuse
6 She ...... for losing the scarf.
  a took responsibility b made up an excuse

B ▶ 1:20 **LISTEN TO SUPPORT AN OPINION** Listen again. After each conversation, discuss whether you think each person did the right thing. What would *you* have done in each situation? Explain why.

"She definitely did the right thing. She took responsibility and offered to pay for the repair. I would have done the same thing. However, if I were the man, I'm not sure I would have accepted her offer."

DIGITAL INDUCTIVE ACTIVITY

C **GRAMMAR "COMMENT" CLAUSES**

An adjective clause beginning with which can be used to modify—or comment on—an independent clause.

He broke his sister's camera, **which made him feel terrible**.
She blamed Paul for causing the accident, **which was totally unfair**.
I had avoided taking responsibility, **which was embarrassing**, so I just made up an excuse.

Comment clauses are non-restrictive—that is, they provide additional information that is not essential to the meaning of the sentence. Use a comma before a comment clause and after it if something else follows.

Be careful!
You cannot use that in place of which in a comment clause:
She always borrows Bob's tablet, **which** really bugs him.
NOT She always borrows Bob's tablet, ~~that~~ really bugs him.

GRAMMAR BOOSTER p. 130
Reduced adjective clauses

DIGITAL MORE EXERCISES

D **GRAMMAR PRACTICE** Write sentences that include comment clauses with which.

Example: Mark is going to replace my camera. (It's really thoughtful of him.)
Mark is going to replace my camera, which is really thoughtful of him.

1 Lena insists on paying for the tickets I gave her. (It's just unnecessary.)
....
2 Mona never returned the book I lent her. (It really bothers me.)
....
3 Apparently, replacing Nancy's ring would cost an arm and a leg. (It's just ridiculous.)
....
4 I offered to pay for dinner. (It was the right thing to do, in my opinion.)
....
5 Gerry crossed the street in the middle of the block. (It's against the law and dangerous.)
....
....

PRONUNCIATION BOOSTER p. 144
Emphatic stress and pitch to express emotion

NOW YOU CAN Express regret and take responsibility

A ▶ 1:21 **CONVERSATION SPOTLIGHT** Read and listen. Notice the spotlighted conversation strategies.

A: Tim, you know that tablet you lent me? Well, **I'm really sorry, but** I have some bad news. I broke it.

B: Oh, no. How did that happen?

A: Well, I tripped and dropped it, which was completely my fault. I feel awful about it.

B: Are you sure it can't be fixed?

A: Pretty sure. I took it to the store, and they said it wouldn't be worth it. I'm going to get you a new one, **if that's OK**.

B: **That's really not necessary**. I was just about to get a new one anyway.

A: No, I insist. It's no problem. And **please accept my apology**.

▶ 1:23 **Ways to express regret**
I feel awful (about it).
I feel (just) terrible.
I'm so sorry.

B ▶ 1:22 **RHYTHM AND INTONATION** Listen again and repeat. Then practice the conversation with a partner.

C **NOTEPADDING** Choose two situations from the survey on page 14 that have actually happened in your life. Make notes about what happened and what you said and did. Use "comment" clauses when possible.

Situation 1: *I forgot a friend's birthday, which was embarrassing.*

Situation 1:	Situation 2:
What I said:	What I said:
What I did:	What I did:

DIGITAL VIDEO
DIGITAL SPEAKING BOOSTER

D **CONVERSATION ACTIVATOR** Create a conversation similar to the one in Exercise A. Start like this: *I'm afraid I have some bad news ...* Be sure to change roles and then partners.

RECYCLE THIS LANGUAGE

- messed up big time
- got carried away
- let things get out of hand
- admit making a mistake
- make up an excuse
- tell the truth
- tell a lie
- shift the blame to someone else
- take responsibility
- avoid taking responsibility
- So what?
- That's not the worst of it.

E **DISCUSSION** Choose one of the situations you wrote about on your notepad. Tell your classmates about what happened and details about what you said and did. Then say whether or not you're satisfied with the outcome and why.

DON'T STOP!

- Continue to negotiate how you'll make up for what happened.
- Say as much as you can.

LESSON 3 **GOAL** Explore where values come from

A **READING WARM-UP** Where do you think people learn the difference between right and wrong? What are the most important lessons children need to learn?

DIGITAL STRATEGIES **B** ▶ 1:24 **READING** Read the article. Which influences do you think are the most important?

THE DEVELOPMENT OF VALUES

We all live by a set of principles or beliefs that guide our actions and help us distinguish between what is morally acceptable or unacceptable. But where do our values come from? In fact, they develop throughout our lives and originate from a variety of sources. Here are some key influences:

PARENTS From earliest childhood, most of us learn a sense of right and wrong from our parents. When they tell us children's stories, we learn simple morals—life lessons about the consequences of good and bad behavior. Our parents correct us when we make mistakes. More importantly, we learn from our parents' actions. Children see everything. They observe how their parents relate to each other and handle social situations, and they always notice whether their parents are truthful or not.

PEERS From childhood through adulthood, our everyday conversations with our friends, classmates, colleagues, neighbors, and acquaintances play a role in developing our moral outlook. We are strongly affected by the views of our peers. We naturally "categorize" the people we know or who we hear about on the news—for instance, who is unfriendly, who is generous, which politicians or celebrities are honest.

RELIGION AND CULTURE Many people attribute their moral principles to their religious upbringing. Religion can provide a clear set of guidelines to live by that make it easier to distinguish between right and wrong. All the world's religions offer values that can move us away from being self-centered toward helping others. The dominant values of the group, community, or culture we grow up in are also a powerful influence on our own worldview. For example, more importance may be placed on conforming to society than on the individual, which affects the choices we make in life.

INSTITUTIONS We also pick up values from the code of ethics promoted by our school, profession, or company. Some schools take a public stand against students' bullying their classmates, which sets a clear principle for how students should behave. A corporation might establish a mission statement for all its employees to follow. In such cases, the company expects employees to make its values part of their personal values.

LIFE EVENTS Significant life events, such as the death of a loved one, a divorce, an accident, or an illness, can shape our sense of ethics. Perhaps a loved one falls gravely ill. Having to take care of a sick relative teaches us about setting priorities and the value of selflessness. A sudden financial loss may force us to re-examine and rethink what is important to us. We might be the victim of a major accident or a natural disaster. Surviving such an event teaches us about the miracle and fragility of life and helps us see—and appreciate—each day differently from the way we did before the event.

Sometimes we face an ethical dilemma in which we have to choose between two opposing values. For example, a close friend may ask us to tell a lie in order to avoid his or her getting in trouble, which presents us with a conflict. While we believe it's important to protect the ones we love, our values also may place great importance on remaining truthful. It's the combined lessons we have learned throughout our lives that help us make the right (or wrong) choices.

C **RELATE TO PERSONAL EXPERIENCE** Complete the chart. Identify one or more values you learned from each of the influences mentioned in the Reading.

Your parents
They taught me to work hard.

Your parents	Your school, profession, or company
Your peers	**Your life events**
Your religion or culture	**Other**

D **CLASSIFY VOCABULARY USING CONTEXT** Cross out the one word that doesn't belong with the other three in each group of words. Explain your answers, based on how the words are used in the article.

1 values	events	beliefs	guidelines
2 peers	acquaintances	celebrities	colleagues
3 a situation	a divorce	an accident	a life event
4 ethics	priorities	morals	principles
5 moral	ethical	right	self-centered

E **CRITICAL THINKING** Read each quote from the article and discuss the questions.

1 "[Children] observe how their parents relate to each other and handle social situations, and they always notice whether their parents are truthful or not."

How do you think children develop values from their observations?

2 "A sudden financial loss may force us to re-examine and rethink what is important to us."

In what ways could a financial loss affect our values?

3 "Sometimes we face an ethical dilemma in which we have to choose between two opposing values."

In addition to the one mentioned in the article, what are some other examples of ethical dilemmas?

DIGITAL EXTRA CHALLENGE

NOW YOU CAN Explore where values come from

A **FRAME YOUR IDEAS** Where do you think your values mostly come from? Rank the following influences in the order of importance in your life, from 1 to 10, with 1 being the most important. Include an "other" if necessary.

	my mother		my colleagues or classmates		my culture
	my father		my teachers		a life event
	other relatives		my school or job		other:
	my friends		my religion		

B **PAIR WORK** Take turns explaining the most important influences on the development of your own values. Provide specific examples. Refer to the chart you completed in Exercise C on page 20. Ask your partner questions.

"The religious teaching I got as a child was, I think, the strongest influence on me. Those are the guidelines that help me remember the difference between right and wrong."

"When I was just a kid, my dad got very sick and he couldn't work. We all had to help take care of my dad. My mom and my oldest sister both worked, so it was a lot harder for both of them. It made me realize how important family is."

LESSON 4 **GOAL** Discuss how best to help others

DIGITAL STRATEGIES **A** ▶ 1:25 **VOCABULARY PHILANTHROPIC WORK** Read and listen. Then listen again and repeat.

do•nor /ˈdoʊnɚ/ *n.* a person or organization that gives money for a specific cause or charity ALSO **do•na•tion** *n. A number of donors have chosen to make their contributions privately. They prefer not to have their names associated with their donations.*

phi•lan•thro•pist /fɪˈlænθrəpɪst/ *n.* a wealthy person who donates a significant amount of his or her money, time, and / or reputation to charitable causes ALSO **phi•lan•thro•py** *n.*, **phi•lan•thro•pic** *adj. A number of celebrities have gotten deeply involved in philanthropy. As philanthropists, they have become almost as famous for their philanthropic work as for their work as actors, singers, and athletes.*

hu•man•i•tar•i•an /hyuˌmænəˈtɛriən/ *n.* a person who is dedicated to improving people's living conditions and treatment by others ALSO hu•man•i•tar•i•an *adj.*, **hu•man•i•tar•i•an•ism** *n. Many celebrities choose to make humanitarianism an important part of their lives. In some cases, they discover that humanitarian work takes up even more of their time—that being a humanitarian can be a full-time job.*

ac•tiv•ist /ˈæktəvɪst/ *n.* a person who works hard for social or political change, often as a member of a social or political organization ALSO **ac•tiv•ism** *n. His activism has often gotten him into trouble. As a political activist, he comes into conflict with those who do not share his views.*

B **ACTIVATE THE VOCABULARY** Read the biographies. Use the Vocabulary to write a sentence about each person and his or her work.

Graça Machel

Graça Machel, the widow of two presidents of two countries—Mozambique and South Africa—is known for her work protecting the rights of child refugees. She currently works to improve children's health.

Li Ka-shing

Hong Kong businessman Li Ka-shing is considered to be the wealthiest man in Asia. A number of universities have benefited from the numerous multi-million dollar contributions from his Li Ka-shing Foundation.

Helen Caldicott

In an effort to protect the environment for the future, Australian physician Helen Caldicott has worked for decades to oppose the use and spread of nuclear weapons and the use of nuclear power.

C **LISTENING WARM-UP** When someone achieves wealth and fame, do you think it's that person's responsibility to donate time and money to help others? Explain your point of view.

DIGITAL STRATEGIES **D** ▶ 1:26 **LISTEN FOR MAIN IDEAS** Listen to Part 1 of a report on celebrity philanthropic work. Choose the best title for it.

☐ **1** Many celebrities try to change the world.
☐ **2** Two celebrities try to make a difference.
☐ **3** Jolie and Bono are highly successful in their chosen careers.
☐ **4** Philanthropic work teaches celebrities new skills.

E ▶ 1:27 **LISTEN TO CLASSIFY** Read the following philanthropic activities. Listen to Part 1 again and write J for Jolie's activities and B for Bono's, according to the report.

1 ...... donates money to build schools.
2 ...... organizes events to raise money.
3 ...... works to protect wildlife.
4 ...... gets world leaders to work together.
5 ...... works to improve medical care.
6 ...... works with the United Nations.

F ▶ 1:28 **LISTEN TO CONFIRM CONTENT** Listen to Part 1 again. Cross out the reasons for celebrity philanthropy that are NOT mentioned.

1 to develop new skills
2 to get attention from the media
3 to satisfy a desire to help end human suffering
4 to show gratitude for one's success
5 to increase one's fame and wealth
6 to change how one is seen by others
7 to address one's concerns about the future

G ▶ 1:29 **LISTEN FOR POINT OF VIEW** Now listen to Part 2. Which statement best represents the speaker's point of view? Explain your answer.

☐ 1 Celebrity philanthropists are only interested in their own fame and getting "photo ops."
☐ 2 While the criticism may have some truth, Jolie's and Bono's philanthropy has been mainly positive.
☐ 3 Despite their good work, Jolie's and Bono's philanthropy deserves a lot of criticism.

H ▶ 1:30 **LISTEN TO SUMMARIZE** Listen to Part 2 again. With a partner, write at least five criticisms of celebrity philanthropists from the report on a separate sheet of paper.

I **SUPPORT AN OPINION** Do celebrities make good philanthropists? Explain. Use information from the report or about other celebrity philanthropists you are aware of.

NOW YOU CAN Discuss how best to help others

A **FRAME YOUR IDEAS** Which three of the issues in the photos on page 22 do you think most urgently need attention? Write them on the notepad and write one activity that would help for each one.

1.	2.	3.

DIGITAL SPEAKING BOOSTER

B **DISCUSSION** Discuss the best activities for solving one of the problems on your notepad.

"I feel strongly about helping children, so I think it's crucial to provide good schools and ..."

OPTIONAL WRITING Do rich and famous people have a responsibility to donate fame and money to help others? Write at least two paragraphs, supporting your point of view.

WRITING Restrictive and non-restrictive adjective clauses

A **WRITING SKILL** Study the rules.

Restrictive adjective clauses

A restrictive adjective clause provides *essential information* necessary to identify the noun or pronoun it modifies. Do not use commas.

The person **who borrowed my camera yesterday** just told me she had broken it.
She replaced the camera lens **that she had broken the day before**.
The friend **whose phone I lost** insisted I didn't need to replace it.
The hotel in the town **where we stayed last weekend** offered to give us a refund.

Non-restrictive adjective clauses

A non-restrictive adjective clause provides *additional information* that is not necessary to identify the noun or pronoun it modifies. Use commas before and after, except at the end of a sentence, when the adjective clause ends with a period.

Lara**, who works in my office,** told me she broke the camera that she had borrowed.

The Aimes Hotel**, where we always get a room in July,** offered to give us a refund.

She replaced the tablet**, which made her very happy.**

My laptop**, which was always crashing when I really needed it,** finally died.

Be careful!
Use punctuation that supports your intended meaning.
The laptop **which I bought last week** is great. (Differentiates this laptop from others: essential)
The laptop, **which I bought last week,** is great. (An additional comment about the laptop: not essential)

B **PRACTICE** Read the college application essay, in which the writer describes a life lesson. Correct punctuation errors with adjective clauses. Add three commas and delete three.

What I Learned from My First Job

While working at my first job which was at a clothing store, I had a co-worker who got me into a lot of trouble. When the manager counted the money in the cash register, it had come up short. The co-worker had taken some of the money, so she shifted the blame to me. I insisted that I wasn't responsible, but the manager who didn't know me fired me immediately.

Ten years later, I got a phone call, that really surprised me. It was from the woman, who had blamed me for taking the money. She called me to apologize for what she had done. Apparently it had been bothering her for a long time.

This incident taught me an important lesson. Sometimes when people tell a lie, they hurt themselves more than the other person. While I had completely forgotten about the incident, it was my former co-worker, who felt badly about it for all those years.

C **PRACTICE** Decide if the adjective clause provides essential or additional information. Write a checkmark if the punctuation is correct. Make corrections if it is a non-restrictive clause.

☐ **1** His grandparents are the ones who taught him the most about right and wrong.

☐ **2** My cousin who was always truthful about everything told my aunt she was wrong.

☐ **3** I told a lie that I have regretted for more than ten years.

☐ **4** Her favorite vase which her mother had given her had been broken.

☐ **5** We found out that Megan was going to join us which was great.

DIGITAL WRITING PROCESS

D **APPLY THE WRITING SKILL** On a separate sheet of paper, write a college application essay in which you describe an experience that taught you a life lesson or that shaped your values. Provide details by including at least three adjective clauses to add essential and additional information.

SELF-CHECK

☐ Did I include at least three adjective clauses?
☐ Did I distinguish between essential and additional information?
☐ Did I use commas correctly in non-restrictive adjective clauses?

DIGITAL GAME

REVIEW

A ▶ 1:31 **Listen to each conversation. Then listen again and complete the statements.**

Conversation 1

1 The man is thinking about ....

a shifting the blame   b taking responsibility   c telling the truth

2 The woman suggests ....

a shifting the blame   b making up an excuse   c telling the truth

Conversation 2

3 The woman has decided to ....

a shift the blame   b make up an excuse   c take responsibility

B **Complete the sentences with phrases from the box. Use each phrase only once.**

shift the blame	admit making a mistake	tell the truth	make up an excuse	take responsibility

1 If Matt makes a mistake, he tries to .... to other people in his office so he won't get in trouble with his boss.

2 Dan forgot to prepare his report for the sales meeting, so he decided to .... He told his boss that his computer deleted the file.

3 Alice borrowed Susan's umbrella, but she forgot it on the train. She wanted to take responsibility, but she didn't want to .... , so she just replaced it and didn't say anything to Susan about it.

4 Jane doesn't .... when she does something wrong. Either she makes up an excuse or she doesn't tell the truth about what happened.

5 I really believe that in some situations it's better not to .... , especially when you are protecting someone's feelings. For example, if my grandmother spent all day cooking dinner, but it tasted terrible, I would still tell her it was delicious.

C **Complete the paragraph with the relative pronouns from the box.**

who
which
that
whom
where
when

Nora Richards, with ....(1) I worked for five years, was a person ....(2) could never get her work done on time. I still remember the time ....(3) she asked me to help her write a long report ....(4) was due the next day! The report, on ....(5) she had been working for an entire month, was needed for a business deal with a very important client. The deal, about ....(6) Nora talked all the time (instead of writing the report), fell through, and Nora was fired. There are situations in ....(7) you simply have to meet your deadlines. Nora was one of those people ....(8) fails to understand that the office is a place ....(9) , as the saying says, "Actions speak louder than words."

D **On a separate sheet of paper, complete each statement with your own comment clause, using which. Don't forget to use a comma.**

Example: Some celebrity philanthropists only care about publicity, ...*which I think is a shame*... .

1 Angelina Jolie has received many awards for her philanthropic work… .

2 Most people tell lies to avoid hurting people's feelings… .

3 My brother took responsibility for his mistake… .

4 I made up an excuse for being late to work… .

TEST-TAKING SKILLS BOOSTER p. 152

Web Project: Celebrity Philanthropists
www.english.com/summit3e

UNIT 3

Fears, Hardships, and Heroism

COMMUNICATION GOALS

1 Express frustration, empathy, and encouragement
2 Describe how fear affects you physically
3 Discuss overcoming handicaps and hardships
4 Examine the nature of heroism

PREVIEW

A FRAME YOUR IDEAS Take the self-test. Total your responses.

How chicken are you?

Rate the situations below, according to how scary they are to you, from 1 to 3, with 1 being not scary at all, 2 being somewhat scary, and 3 being very scary.

getting stuck in an elevator	walking outside during a bad storm
seeing a bee on your arm	standing near the edge of a cliff
driving in bad weather	going to the dentist
eating in an unclean restaurant	walking down a dark street at night
riding a horse	experiencing turbulence during a flight
smelling smoke in a building	getting an injection from a doctor or nurse
being a passenger in a speeding car	seeing a snake in your garden
taking a roller-coaster ride	being in a place undergoing an epidemic

YOUR CHICKEN SCORE

TOTAL YOUR SCORE

16–26

You're cool and collected. Nothing freaks you out.

27–37

You're just cautious.

38–48

You're a total chicken! You're probably afraid of your own shadow.

B PAIR WORK Compare self-tests with a partner. Are you both afraid of the same things? Which of you is more chicken?

C GROUP WORK How chicken is your class? Calculate the average score for each situation in your class. Which situation is the most frightening to everyone?

ENGLISH FOR TODAY'S WORLD
Understand a variety of accents.
Luiz = Portuguese
Michel = French

D ▶ 2:02 **SPOTLIGHT** Read and listen to two friends discuss a problem. Notice the spotlighted language.

Luiz: Hey, Michel. Anything wrong? You look like you've lost your best friend.
Michel: No. Nothing like that. I'm just **in hot water** with Emilie.
Luiz: Emilie? But the two of you were so lovey-dovey when I saw you at the restaurant on Sunday. What's up?
Michel: Well, Sunday was her birthday, and we'd been planning to get engaged on her birthday, but I guess I **got cold feet**. I just don't think I'm ready to make that kind of commitment yet. In any case, she's really upset. She feels like I **pulled the rug out from under her**.
Luiz: Well, I can imagine that must have been really disappointing for her. Don't you feel like you're in love anymore? Or is there someone else?
Michel: No. Definitely not. I love her **with all my heart**, but no matter how much I tell myself she's the only one for me, I **just can't take the plunge**. I don't know what's wrong with me. Maybe it's some kind of psychological problem.
Luiz: I wouldn't **jump to that conclusion**. Marriage is **a big deal**, Michel. And it's forever. Most people find that scary.
Michel: I think that's what **freaks me out** about it. Every time I think of proposing, I panic. I feel so guilty that I don't even want to see her right now.
Luiz: Well, **it's not the end of the world**. Sounds like you just **have a minor case of the jitters**.
Michel: You think so?
Luiz: **Mark my words**. She'll wait for you. **Just chill** for a while until you're ready, OK?

E **UNDERSTAND IDIOMS AND EXPRESSIONS** Choose the best way to complete each statement.

1 If you're "in hot water," you're ....
a in trouble **b** excited

2 When you "get cold feet," you ....
a decide to do something as you had planned
b decide not to do something as you had planned

3 If Emilie feels like Michel "pulled the rug out from under her," she feels that ....
a he didn't do what he had promised
b he was disappointed with her

4 If you do something "with all your heart," you do it ....
a unwillingly **b** with 100% commitment

5 When Michel said "I just can't take the plunge," he meant he ....
a couldn't go through with proposing
b didn't want to marry her

6 When Luiz says "I wouldn't jump to that conclusion," he's suggesting that Michel's reasoning is probably ....
a right **b** not right

7 Something that's "a big deal" is ....
a full of advantages **b** of great importance

8 If something "freaks you out," it ....
a scares you **b** excites you

9 If something "isn't the end of the world," it's ....
a not a big deal **b** not good

10 When Luiz says "Sounds like you just have a minor case of the jitters," he means ....
a Michel is just nervous
b Michel should take his doubt seriously

11 When you say "Mark my words," you want someone to ....
a remember your prediction later
b wait for you later

12 When Luiz tells Michel to "just chill," he's suggesting that Michel ....
a do something right away
b wait

SPEAKING **SUMMARIZE AND PERSONALIZE** First, summarize Michel's problem and say what you would do in his situation. Speculate about what will happen next. Then, discuss what scares you more: fears of physical harm such as the ones in the self-test, or emotional fears such as the ones Michel is experiencing. Explain your reasons, using examples from your life.

GOAL Express frustration, empathy, and encouragement

DIGITAL STRATEGIES

A ▶ 2:03 **VOCABULARY EXPRESSING FRUSTRATION, EMPATHY, AND ENCOURAGEMENT**
Read and listen. Then listen again and repeat.

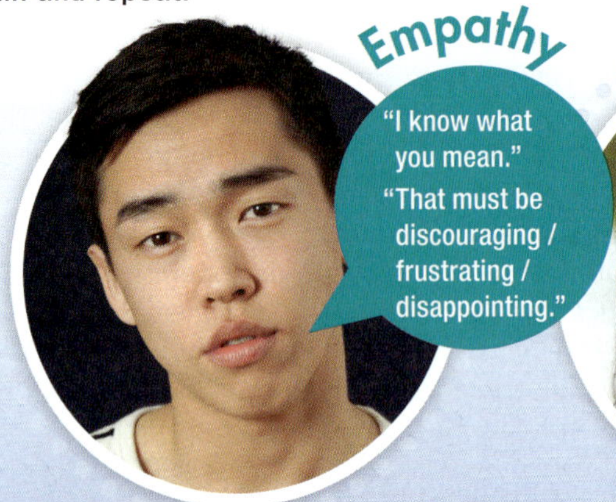

B ▶ 2:04 **LISTEN TO PREDICT** Listen to the conversations. Then choose what the other person will probably say next.

1 a That must be frustrating. b I just can't take it anymore.
2 a I give up! b I know what you mean.
3 a I've had it! b Well, don't give up.
4 a I'm really fed up! b Don't let it get you down.
5 a Hang in there. b I just can't take it any more!

GRAMMAR BOOSTER p. 131
Embedded questions: review and common errors

DIGITAL INDUCTIVE ACTIVITY

C **GRAMMAR CLAUSES WITH NO MATTER**

Use no matter + a noun clause beginning with a question word to express frustration (that no amount of anything, for example *effort*, can make something change). Use a comma before or after clauses with no matter.

No matter how careful I am, I always forget something!
No matter what they said, he didn't believe them.
No matter what time we check in, we always have to wait for a room.
No one answers, **no matter when we call**.
They can't understand her, **no matter how slowly she speaks**.

Be careful!
Use normal, not inverted, word order in the noun clause and don't use an auxiliary verb.
No matter **who you ask**, no one can give you directions.
NOT No matter ~~who do you ask~~, …

DIGITAL MORE EXERCISES

D **GRAMMAR PRACTICE** Mark correct sentences with a checkmark. Mark incorrect sentences with an X. Correct the incorrect sentences.

[X] 1 No matter how much do I encourage my sister, she won't take a plane anywhere.
No matter how much I encourage my sister, she won't take a plane anywhere.

[ ] 2 Eric couldn't find his folder, no matter how hard did he look.
....

[ ] 3 No matter how late Phil stays up, he still gets up for his exercise class.
....

[ ] 4 They were unable to find a gas station, no matter how many people did they ask.
....

[ ] 5 No matter how many cups of coffee I drink, I sleep like a baby.
....

[ ] 6 No matter when do I go to bed, I always get up tired.
....

E **PAIR WORK** Complete the conversations with your own ideas, using the Vocabulary from page 28. Then read your conversations with a partner.

1 A: .... ! No matter how little I eat, ...
B: ....
2 A: .... ! No matter what I tell my supervisor at work, ...
B: ....
3 A: .... ! I can't find my keys, ...
B: ....
4 A: .... ! Mary is always late, ...
B: ....

PRONUNCIATION BOOSTER p. 145
Vowel reduction to /ə/

NOW YOU CAN Express frustration, empathy, and encouragement

A ▶ 2:05 **CONVERSATION SPOTLIGHT** Read and listen. Notice the spotlighted conversation strategies.

A: Hey, Nina. You look upset. **Is something wrong**?
B: Actually, I've been having a bit of trouble at work.
A: I'm sorry to hear that. **What's going on**?
B: **Well, basically**, no matter how well I do something, my boss never gives me credit.
A: That must be frustrating.
B: It is. I'm feeling really fed up.
A: I totally understand. **Hang in there**, though, OK?
B: Thanks for the encouragement! I appreciate it.
A: **Anytime.**

B ▶ 2:06 **RHYTHM AND INTONATION** Listen again and repeat. Then practice the conversation with a partner.

C **NOTEPADDING** Write statements on the notepad describing problems. Use no matter.

with a relationship: *with my boyfriend. No matter how many times I ask him, he won't be friendly to my friends.*

at home:

at work:

at school:

with money:

with a relationship:

with my health:

DIGITAL VIDEO
DIGITAL SPEAKING BOOSTER

D **CONVERSATION ACTIVATOR** Create a conversation similar to the one in Exercise A. Start like this: *You look upset. Is something wrong?* Use one of the problems from your notepad. Be sure to change roles and then partners.

DON'T STOP!
- Ask for more details about the problem.
- Offer specific advice.
- Say as much as you can.

RECYCLE THIS LANGUAGE
- No way!
- Don't freak out.
- Just chill.
- It's not the end of the world.
- Wish me luck!
- Mark my words.

LESSON 2

GOAL Describe how fear affects you physically

A ▶ 2:07 **GRAMMAR SPOTLIGHT** Read how fear affects people physically. Notice the spotlighted grammar.

Q: What happens to you when you get really scared? What situations usually cause this reaction?

The worst thing for me is that I get sweaty palms and my hands shake. The first time I met my fiancée's parents, we were at a nice restaurant and my hands were shaking **so badly that** I avoided even picking up my glass. I was afraid they would think I had some kind of disease. I wish I could control this, but I can't. It's so embarrassing!

Kenji Yaegashi, 28 Nagoya, Japan

I get **such terrible palpitations that** it feels like my heart's going to jump right out of my chest. And when things are really bad, I can actually lose my voice. Fortunately, this only happens when I'm really panicked, like the time I was on a flight and the landing gear got stuck. I tried to pretend I was cool and collected, but the truth is I was terrified.

Jorge Pardo, 32 Cuenca, Ecuador

Having to speak English on the phone! I know it's crazy because I speak pretty well. But there's just something about it that makes me panic. It's **so bad that** when I know I have to make a call in English, I get **such awful butterflies in my stomach that** I think I'm going to get sick. Silly, I know, but true. But actually, once I start talking the butterflies go away.

Isil Farat, 24 Izmir, Turkey

B **RELATE TO PERSONAL EXPERIENCE** Which situation described in the Grammar Spotlight do you identify with most? Explain, providing examples from your own life.

GRAMMAR BOOSTER p. 132
Count and non-count nouns:
- Non-count nouns made countable
- Nouns used in countable and uncountable sense

DIGITAL INDUCTIVE ACTIVITY

C **GRAMMAR USING SO ... (THAT) OR SUCH ... (THAT) TO EXPLAIN RESULTS**

Use so to intensify an adjective or an adverb to explain the result of an extreme situation. That is optional. Don't use a comma.

extreme situation	result
It was **so stormy**	**(that)** I was afraid to get on the plane.
She left **so quickly**	**(that)** she forgot her umbrella.

If the adjective is followed directly by a noun, use such, not so.

I was wearing **such uncomfortable shoes (that)** I could hardly walk.
I made **such salty soup (that)** no one could eat it.
She had **such a bad accident (that)** she never drove again.

If the noun is preceded by many, much, few, or little, use so.

There will be **so many people** there **(that)** we won't be able to find each other.
There was **so much lightning (that)** all the passengers on the plane were terrified.
We ate **so few meals** out last month **(that)** we saved a lot of money.
There's **so little ice** on the road **(that)** I think it's safe to drive.

Be careful!
Always use a or an with a singular count noun following such.
She had **such a bad accident** that she never drove again.
NOT She had ~~so bad accident~~ that she never drove again.

Remember: Use many and few with count nouns. Use much and little with non-count nouns.
He had **so many tickets** that he lost his driver's license.
NOT He had ~~so much tickets~~ that he lost his driver's license.

DIGITAL MORE EXERCISES

D GRAMMAR PRACTICE On a separate sheet of paper, combine the statements, using so … (that) or such … (that).

The fire was so terrible that the building was totally destroyed.

1 The fire was terrible. The building was totally destroyed.
2 There are usually many accidents. We don't travel on holiday weekends.
3 The games end late. We prefer to watch them on TV.
4 The insects are awful after dark. Most people prefer to stay inside in the evening.
5 Traffic in this region has become a bad problem. Lots of people are taking public transportation.
6 It was a stormy day. We postponed our picnic.

E GRAMMAR PRACTICE Complete each statement with much, little, many, or few.

1 They cancelled so .... flights that we won't be able to get there tonight.
2 There's always so .... trouble when the weather is bad that we don't travel in winter.
3 So .... people ate at that restaurant that they had to close it.
4 There were so .... seats left on the train that my friends and I couldn't sit together.
5 There was so .... time to get to the shelter that we just stayed in our basement.

DIGITAL STRATEGIES

F ▶ 2:08 **VOCABULARY PHYSICAL EFFECTS OF FEAR** Read and listen. Then listen again and repeat.

My hands shake.

I get palpitations.

I get sweaty palms.

I get butterflies in my stomach.

G ACTIVATE THE VOCABULARY Find and underline the Vocabulary and other physical effects of fear in the Grammar Spotlight. Paraphrase the situation that caused the physical effect for each of the three people, using the Vocabulary in your description.

“Jorge Pardo was so scared that he got palpitations and he lost his voice.”

NOW YOU CAN Describe how fear affects you physically

A NOTEPADDING Choose a time when you were so scared that it affected you physically. Write notes about it on the notepad. Use the grammar and Vocabulary from page 30.

What I was afraid of:

How it affected me physically:

Write one statement with so or such … (that).

What finally happened?

DIGITAL VIDEO

B DISCUSSION ACTIVATOR Discuss the situations on your notepads. Tell each other your stories, asking for more information and details. Idea: Tell the class about what happened to your partner. Say as much as you can.

RECYCLE THIS LANGUAGE
- No matter …
- Did you freak out?
- It wasn't the end of the world.

OPTIONAL WRITING Write your partner's story. Use sequencing expressions (first, next, after that, etc.) to clarify the order of events in his or her story.

LESSON 3 **GOAL** Discuss overcoming handicaps and hardships

A **READING WARM-UP** What are some physical handicaps people face? What are some other hardships that might limit people's ability to succeed?

DIGITAL STRATEGIES **B** ▶ 2:09 **READING** Read about Marlee Matlin. If you had to choose one adjective to describe her, what would it be?

THE COURAGE TO BE WHO SHE IS

Marlee Matlin, the only deaf performer ever to win the Oscar for Best Actress in a Leading Role, is also known worldwide as a stage and TV actor, an author, and as a spokesperson for people with hearing disabilities. Through her work and her books she has devoted her life to encouraging children and adults with hearing loss to live normal lives with normal expectations.

Born with normal hearing, Marlee suffered permanent hearing loss at 18 months from an illness with a high fever. As she approached school age, her parents were advised to send her to a specialized boarding school far from home. However, her parents felt that Marlee would be deprived of the parental contact and love essential to normal development if she didn't live at home. So instead, they put her in a public mainstream school that had both hearing and deaf students, which built her confidence to participate in activities with hearing students. At school, Marlee learned sign language, though she was encouraged to use her voice, too.

Throughout her childhood, Marlee's parents did everything they could to give her the same life she would have had if she had had normal hearing. Her family even helped Marlee develop a sense of humor about herself so she wouldn't be ashamed of her handicap. When others wondered about the strange way she pronounced some words (because she had learned to say them without ever having *heard* them), her brother would say she had an accent because she was from a foreign country, which made both of them laugh.

At seven, her parents enrolled her in a summer camp with both hearing and deaf children, and there she learned to use her hands to "sign" the lyrics of songs as the other children sang. Her campmates loved this, and their applause gave Marlee her first taste of the joy of performing.

To encourage her, when Marlee returned home from camp, her mother enrolled her in an afterschool children's theater program (now called the International Center on Deafness and the Arts, or ICODA), where children prepared some performances in sign language and others in spoken English.

Matlin continued performing when she was in college. At one performance, the popular TV actor Henry Winkler was in the audience. Matlin approached him and said she wanted to be a famous actor like him. Winkler, who suffers from dyslexia (a reading disorder that causes difficulty in reading despite normal intelligence), empathized with Matlin and encouraged her, telling her she could be anything she wanted and not to let anything stand in her way. Winkler became a longtime mentor and friend to Matlin, helping her as she pursued her acting career.

Matlin's life hasn't been without controversy or criticism. When presenting an Oscar, she spoke the nominees' names instead of signing them, causing some deaf people to complain she was suggesting *they* should speak instead of signing. To comfort Matlin, African-American actor Whoopi Goldberg told her that once she had worn blue contact lenses just for fun and was criticized for trying to "appear white." Goldberg told Matlin not to worry about what others say and just be herself.

Matlin has never let her handicap stand in her way and has continued to surpass the expectations the public has of people who can't hear. When she competed in TV's *Dancing with the Stars*, people were incredulous: How could she dance if she couldn't hear the music?

The key to Matlin's success may, in part, lie in the support and help others have given her—support that has enabled Matlin to be who she is, no matter what others may believe or say.

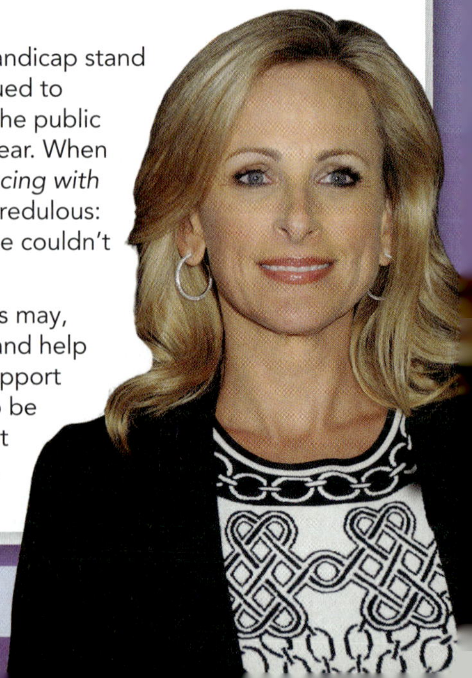

Marlee Matlin has never let her handicap stand in her way.

C UNDERSTAND MEANING FROM CONTEXT Match the words and phrases from the article with these definitions. Then, with a partner, write sentences using the terms.

1 a person who represents and speaks for a group of people
2 a system of communication using hand gestures
3 a physical or mental disability or a condition that can limit a person's ability to function normally
4 an advisor from whom someone receives support and encouragement
5 strong differences of opinion, especially between groups of people

mentor
spokesperson
handicap
conflicts
sign language

D SUMMARIZE In the chart, summarize how these people and institutions contributed to Matlin's development and success. Then compare summaries with your classmates.

	Ways in which they helped Matlin
Her parents	
Her school	
Her brother	
Her summer camp	
Henry Winkler	
Whoopi Goldberg	

E DISCUSSION Discuss the following questions.

1 How do you think a person can learn to speak without ever hearing others speak?
2 In your opinion, what are some general factors that contribute to the success of people who have handicaps or other problems that could limit their success in life?

DIGITAL EXTRA CHALLENGE

NOW YOU CAN Discuss overcoming handicaps and hardships

A FRAME YOUR IDEAS Choose a historical figure, a fictional character, or someone you know who overcame or has overcome a handicap or other hardship. Write discussion notes.

IDEAS: Some types of hardships
- a physical or mental handicap
- racial, ethnic, or sexual discrimination
- a natural disaster
- political instability or war
- poverty, lack of education or family support

Name:

Summary of handicap or hardship:

Factors that helped him or her overcome it:

Achievements:

She has overcome her handicap by playing tennis in a wheelchair.

DIGITAL SPEAKING BOOSTER

B DISCUSSION Compare information. What similarities do the people share? Explain.

LESSON 4

GOAL Examine the nature of heroism

DIGITAL STRATEGIES **A** 2:10 **LISTENING WARM-UP WORD STUDY USING PARTS OF SPEECH** Study the forms of these words related to bravery and heroism, according to the part of speech. (Check meaning of any unfamiliar words in a dictionary.) Read and listen. Then listen again and repeat.

adjective	adverb	noun
brave	bravely	bravery
confident	confidently	confidence
courageous	courageously	courage
fearless	fearlessly	fearlessness
heroic	heroically	heroism
willing	willingly	willingness

DIGITAL STRATEGIES **B** 2:11 **LISTEN TO ACTIVATE PARTS OF SPEECH** Listen to a TV news magazine story. Use a word from the Word Study chart in the correct part of speech to complete each statement. Some items have more than one possible answer.

1 Seol's decision to go back to the plane wreckage was extremely ....

2 Although aware that the airplane could explode at any moment, Seol .... returned to the plane again and again to rescue wounded passengers.

3 Seol's .... to risk his life to save others was extraordinary.

4 The story suggests that anyone, even an apparently ordinary person, is capable of .... acts.

5 Most people don't have the .... to act in the way Seol Ik Soo did.

Rescue personnel look for victims in the wreckage of an airliner.

C 2:12 **LISTEN FOR DETAILS** Listen to the story again. Complete each statement.

1 Seol carried ...... passengers out of the plane.
 a three b more than three

2 During the rescue, Seol felt as if the passengers were very ....
 a heavy b light

3 Seol used a ...... to make bandages.
 a belt b shirt

4 ...... he took passengers out of the plane, he realized that there was blood on his face.
 a Before b After

5 Before the crash, ... thought of Seol as a hero.
 a no one had ever b everyone had always

D ▶ 2:13 **LISTEN TO RETELL A STORY** Listen to the story again. Retell the story in writing, including the important details and using at least three of the words from the Word Study chart. Exchange stories with a partner and suggest details your partner may have left out.

NOW YOU CAN Examine the nature of heroism

A **NOTEPADDING** Frame your ideas. With a partner, discuss and write your own description of the behavior that makes someone a hero. Use words from the Word Study chart and other phrases.

A hero is someone who ...

RECYCLE THIS LANGUAGE

- hangs in there
- doesn't give up
- doesn't freak out
- No matter what happens

B **DISCUSSION** Read the three profiles. Which person's behavior comes closest to the description you wrote in Exercise A. Explain and discuss with a partner.

DAILY NEWS

ROSA PARKS

Rosa Parks on the Montgomery bus.

In 1955, Rosa Parks got on a city bus in Montgomery, a city in the southern U.S., and sat down in a seat near the front. In those days, buses in Montgomery were racially segregated, and the front 10 seats were permanently reserved for white passengers. The driver told her to move to the back, but Parks refused. The driver then called the police, and she was arrested and taken to jail. Rosa Parks's act of defiance took great courage because of the brutality and injustice African Americans faced at that time in the South of the U.S. Her arrest became a rallying point, and the African-American community organized a bus boycott that lasted 381 days, during which no African American rode a city bus in Montgomery. Parks's action had a powerful economic impact on the bus company, which was forced to change its policy. Ultimately through the efforts of the community, racial segregation of public buses was made illegal.

Dr. Sheikh Umar Khan

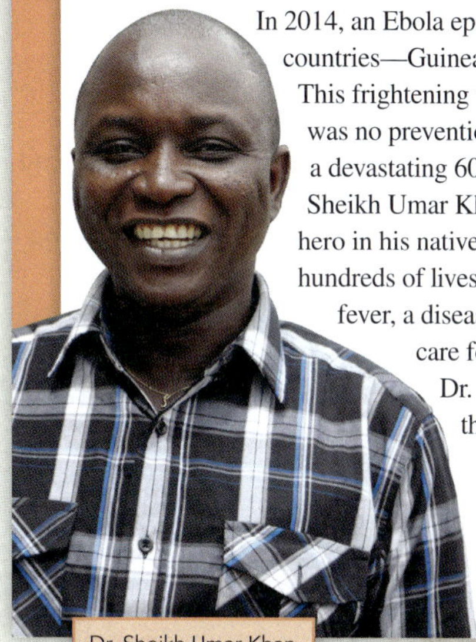

Dr. Sheikh Umar Khan

In 2014, an Ebola epidemic raged in three African countries—Guinea, Liberia, and Sierra Leone. This frightening viral disease, for which there was no prevention or treatment, typically killed a devastating 60% to 90% of those infected. Dr. Sheikh Umar Khan, already hailed as a medical hero in his native Sierra Leone for having saved hundreds of lives during 10 years of battling Lassa fever, a disease similar to Ebola, rushed in to care for more than 100 Ebola patients. Dr. Khan knew better than anyone else that the people at greatest risk were health care workers. In spite of taking precautions, Dr. Khan and three of the nurses who worked with him died of the virus within three days of each other.

Alicia Sorohan

On October 11, while camping in Queensland, Australia, Alicia Sorohan awoke to the sound of someone screaming. Rushing out of her tent, she came across her friend Mike Kerr in the mouth of a 4.2-meter saltwater crocodile. The 60-year-old grandmother immediately jumped on the back of the giant crocodile, which dropped Kerr and attacked her, biting her in the face and arm. When shot and killed by another member of the group, the crocodile had Sorohan's arm in its mouth and was dragging her into the water. Sorohan and Kerr both survived the incident though both had serious injuries. Family members of the victims, in shock after the horrible attack, said that Sorohan's speedy response had been astonishing. "She deserves an award of some kind," said Wayne Clancy, her son-in-law.

a giant saltwater crocodile

C **DEBATE** From pages 34 and 35, choose the person you consider to be the most heroic. Meet with two or three other classmates, each of whom has chosen someone different. Have a debate about which of the persons is the most heroic. Decide among yourselves or among the other students in the class who won the debate.

WRITING Reducing adverbial clauses

A WRITING SKILL Study the rules.

Reducing adverbial clauses to adverbial phrases

Adverbial clauses can be reduced to adverbial phrases when the subject of the independent clause and the adverbial clause are the same. Reduced adverbial phrases are more common in writing than in speaking.

Adverbial clauses	→	Reduced to adverbial phrases
When I fell off my bike, I hurt my back.	→	**Falling off my bike**, I hurt my back.
When we were eating, we got a call.	→	**When eating** (or **Eating**), we got a call.
We saw a bear **while we were hiking**.	→	We saw a bear **while hiking**.
Before I left, I sent my parents a letter.	→	**Before leaving**, I sent my parents a letter.
After I had shared my news, I felt better.	→	**After having shared my news**, I felt better.

Be careful!

When the subjects of the adverbial clause and the independent clause are different, the clause can't be reduced.

Before **she** saw the crocodile, **it** attacked.

DON'T SAY ~~Before seeing the crocodile~~, it attacked.

Punctuation

Use a comma after a clause or phrase when it comes first.

Before I left, I sent my parents a letter. / I sent my parents a letter **before I left.**

B PRACTICE Read the short news report to the right of a frightening event. Underline the reduced adverbial phrases and, on a separate sheet of paper, rewrite the sentences with them, changing the phrases to clauses.

C PRACTICE On a separate sheet of paper, rewrite each of the following sentences, reducing adverbial clauses to adverbial phrases when possible. If the sentence can't be reduced, explain why not.

1 When she was waking up, Alicia Sorohan heard a scream.

2 While Dr. Khan was trying to save his patients, several nurses on his staff came down with Ebola.

3 When she refused to move to the back seats on the bus, Rosa Parks was arrested.

4 Before she went to the drama program, Marlee Matlin hadn't ever performed in a play.

5 Seol realized that he was covered in blood after he had exited the plane several times.

WRITING MODEL

May 5—While camping yesterday, the Evans family was surprised by some frightening neighbors: a bear cub and its mother. Twin 5-year-olds Paul and Marcy were delighted because the young animal reminded them of the cute creatures in their picture books and on TV. Their father, on the other hand, wasn't as charmed because he knew that approaching a bear cub was dangerous since an adult bear is usually nearby.

Luckily for the family, Mr. Evans was already awake and getting breakfast ready when he heard the bear. As he posted later on Facebook: "While getting the milk out of our camping bag, I heard a rustling noise behind me. I turned around and saw a bear cub trying to open the garbage can. I knew I had to think fast."

Hearing his kids coming out of the tent, Mr. Evans quickly pushed them back inside to prevent them from approaching the bear to play with it. At that moment, a large adult female, probably the cub's mother, came by and led the cub away. The Evanses' camping day continued peacefully after that.

DIGITAL WRITING PROCESS

D APPLY THE WRITING SKILL Write a short report about a dangerous or frightening event, using the Writing Model for support. Write at least two paragraphs and tell the story in the order that the events occurred. The event can be real or fictional. Use at least three adverbial clauses and phrases to clarify time relationships.

SELF-CHECK

- ☐ Did I write two or more paragraphs?
- ☐ Does my report tell the story in the order that the events occurred?
- ☐ Did I use at least three adverbial clauses or reduced adverbial phrases to clarify time relationships?

DIGITAL GAME

REVIEW

A ▶ 2:14 **Listen to each person. Then listen again to summarize each person's reason for being frustrated. Write statements with no matter.**

Felix Tan

....

....

....

Robert Reston

....

....

....

Eva García

....

....

....

B Complete each statement with no matter and who, whom, when, what time, what, where, or how.

1 I always get up at seven in the morning, ... I go to bed.
2 My daughter won't go to bed early, ... many times I tell her to.
3 .... the weather is like, we're going!
4 .... few calories you eat, it's hard to lose weight.
5 No one knew which gate the train was leaving from, ... we asked.
6 .... you leave from, the trip still takes two hours.

C Complete each statement with the correct word.

1 The thunder was (so / such) loud that we couldn't sleep.
2 The kids ate (so much / such many) candy that they got sick.
3 There was (so / such) bad turbulence that the passengers couldn't leave their seats.
4 The store has (so many / so much) brands of painkillers that I don't know which to buy.
5 Lyn is having (so / such a) good time at the party that she doesn't want to go home.
6 He learned Italian (so / such) quickly that he took the exam after only two months.

D Replace each underlined word with a word that has a similar meaning and the correct part of speech.

1 Many people don't think they are courageous until they are faced with an emergency.
   a fearlessly **b** brave **c** heroism
2 Few people are fearless enough to fight an adult bear.
   a courageous **b** confidence **c** willing
3 Bravery, especially in dangerous situations, is a rare quality.
   a Courageous **b** Heroism **c** Heroically

E On a separate sheet of paper, create a two-line conversation for each pair of expressions. Use no matter and your own ideas.

1 I'm fed up. / Hang in there.
2 I just can't take it anymore. / Don't let it get you down.
3 I've had it. / That must be discouraging.
4 I give up. / Don't let it get you down.
5 I'm fed up. / I know what you mean.

A: I'm fed up. No matter how much exercise I do, I still look like a weakling!
B: Hang in there. It takes time to see results.

TEST-TAKING SKILLS BOOSTER p. 153

Web Project: Heroes
www.english.com/summit3e

UNIT 4 Getting Along with Others

COMMUNICATION GOALS

1 Discuss how to overcome shortcomings
2 Acknowledge inconsiderate behavior
3 Explain how you handle anger
4 Explore the qualities of friendship

PREVIEW

A FRAME YOUR IDEAS Read about some common shortcomings. Rate each person according to the scale:

A = Sounds just like me!
B = Sounds a bit like me.
C = Doesn't sound like me at all!

What's your biggest shortcoming?

Martin ☐

"I wish I weren't so disorganized. My bedroom's always a mess. I can't remember where I've put anything. The way I'm doing things is just not working for me."

Lena ☐

"You know what my problem is? I'm a procrastinator! I'm always putting things off and waiting till the last minute to do things. Then I go into a panic worrying about whether or not I'll be able to finish on time."

Ricardo ☐

"I admit I'm a bit oversensitive. I tend to overreact to things people say to me—I think I'm being criticized when people are just trying to help. It really doesn't take much to get me upset about stuff."

Paul ☐

"I'm sure I'm too hot-tempered. I get angry way too easily. It doesn't take much to set me off. But I've been trying to change that."

Sophie ☐

"I know I'm too negative. I'm always focusing on the bad rather than the good. And I'm way too critical of others. My husband, though, is just the opposite!"

Jean ☐

"My husband says I'm too controlling—and he's probably right. I complain when he doesn't do things *my* way. I'm sure it drives him crazy!

Trevor ☐

"My biggest shortcoming is that I'm a perfectionist. No matter what I do, I'm not satisfied. I just don't think it's good enough. My attitude really gets in my way."

B ▶ 2:15 **VOCABULARY SHORTCOMINGS** Listen and repeat.

- be disorganized
- be a procrastinator
- be oversensitive
- be hot-tempered
- be negative
- be controlling
- be a perfectionist

C PAIR WORK Tell your partner how you are—or aren't—like the people in Exercise A. What are your biggest shortcomings?

"One of my biggest shortcomings is that I'm a perfectionist. I'd like to invite friends for dinner at my house, but I never do—because I don't think I cook well enough."

D DISCUSSION Discuss these questions.

1 Do any of the people above sound like someone you know? In what ways?
2 Can you think of any other common shortcomings people have? What are they?

ENGLISH FOR TODAY'S WORLD
Understand a variety of accents.
Mike = American English (standard)
Jaya = Hindi

E ▶ 2:16 **SPOTLIGHT** Read and listen to a conversation between two colleagues. Notice the spotlighted language.

Mike: Wait till you hear this … Sam **lost his cool** again at the status meeting!
Jaya: Oh, please. He's always angry about something. So what **set him off** this time?
Mike: You know how Rob always waits till the last minute to do the sales report? Well, Sam **made a big issue out of** it. When Rob tried to defend himself, Sam **told him off**—in front of *everyone*.
Jaya: That's awful! You know, even if Rob starts things late, he always finishes on time. I don't see what the big deal is.
Mike: But you know Sam. If there's anything he hates, it's procrastination. I'm sure he wanted to make an example out of Rob.
Jaya: Well, it sounds like he went overboard. He could have just **brought it up** privately with Rob after the meeting.
Mike: Good point. But, all things considered, Rob **took it pretty well**. He knows Sam's just hot-tempered.
Jaya: If only he'd just stop and think first before having one of his outbursts! Instead, everyone always has to **walk on eggshells** wondering who's going to be next.
Mike: I agree. Between you and me, I think Sam's been under a lot of pressure lately from *his* boss. But that's no excuse to **take it out on** someone else.
Jaya: That's right. It must have been hard for everyone at the meeting to just **pick up the pieces** afterwards and go on as if nothing had happened. I'll bet it was really awkward.
Mike: Totally. But it's Sam who should feel awkward. What bothers me the most is that he has no clue how he affects other people.

F UNDERSTAND IDIOMS AND EXPRESSIONS Find these expressions in Spotlight. Complete each statement.

1 If you "lose your cool," you …… .
 a get angry b are worried
2 If something "sets you off," it …… .
 a makes you angry b relaxes you
3 If someone "makes a big issue out of" something, he or she …… it.
 a enjoys talking about
 b calls too much attention to
4 If you "tell someone off," you are expressing your …… to that person about his or her behavior.
 a anger b appreciation
5 If something bothers you and you "bring it up" with someone, you want to …… .
 a discuss it b avoid discussing it
6 If someone gets angry at you and you "take it well," you are …… by it.
 a not very affected b very affected
7 If you "walk on eggshells," you …… make someone angry.
 a try to b are careful not to
8 If you feel stressed and "take it out on" a friend, you might need to apologize to that person for …… .
 a being stressed b acting angry
9 If you try to "pick up the pieces" after an argument, you try to …… .
 a re-establish a friendly atmosphere
 b understand someone's point of view

G THINK AND EXPLAIN With a partner, discuss the questions and explain your answers.

1 Why does Jaya think the other people at the meeting must have felt uncomfortable?
2 Why do you think Rob wasn't upset about the situation?

SPEAKING GROUP WORK Which of the shortcomings from page 38 do you think cause the greatest problems for people? Discuss the consequences.

"In my opinion, being hot-tempered causes the most problems. Once you've gone overboard, it's hard to pick up the pieces."

LESSON 1 **GOAL** Discuss how to overcome shortcomings

A ▶ 2:17 **GRAMMAR SPOTLIGHT** Read about the workshops. Notice the spotlighted grammar.

SELF-HELP FOR THE SELF-CRITICAL

Practical workshops to help you reach your goals!

1 GET ORGANIZED NOW
Tired of being so disorganized? Is it hard to find things **even if you've filed them away properly**? Have papers been piling up on your desk **whether or not you've had time to go through them**? Take the bull by the horns and discover how getting organized can help you increase your productivity today.

2 STOP TRYING TO CONTROL OTHERS
Do you drive people crazy by constantly supervising what they are doing? Does this sound like you: "**Only if things are done my way** will things get done right!" Let's face it—something's got to change. **Otherwise**, no one's ever going to want to work with you! Letting go of control is easier than you think.

3 END NEGATIVE THINKING NOW
Is your negative attitude interfering with your goals in life? Achieving your goals will be possible **only if you make a decision to change your outlook today**. This workshop will move you from the negative to the positive on a journey that will change your life.

4 SAY GOOD-BYE TO PROCRASTINATION
Have you been putting off till tomorrow what you could have done today? **Unless you're the type who says "I'll never change,"** you *too* can learn to stop procrastinating today. Learn easy strategies for using your time more efficiently than ever.

B **PAIR WORK** Do you think people can really overcome their shortcomings? Why or why not? Which of the workshops would you personally find the most useful? Explain.

DIGITAL INDUCTIVE ACTIVITY

C **GRAMMAR** **ADVERB CLAUSES OF CONDITION**

Use even if or whether or not in an adverb clause to express the fact that no matter what the condition, there is no way to affect or change an event or situation.

Even if I have plenty of time to finish a project, I still wait till the last minute to begin.
(= No matter what, I wait till the last minute.)
She would have been late for the meeting **even if she had set her alarm**.
(= No matter what, she would have been late.)
Whether or not anyone says anything to her about it, Kyla's desk is always a disorganized mess.
(= No matter what, her desk is always a mess.)
We would have been uncomfortable at the meeting **whether or not he had lost his cool**.
(= No matter what, we would have been uncomfortable.)

Use only if to express the fact that a certain condition is necessary in order for something to happen or to be true. If the adverb clause comes first, invert the subject and verb (or auxiliary) in the independent clause and do not use a comma.

Nina will be happy at her job **only if she learns to say no to her boss**. OR
Only if Nina learns to say no to her boss **will she** be happy at her job.

Use unless to express the consequence of an action or lack of action. (Note: unless = if ... not)

Unless he writes himself a note, he'll forget to pay his bills.
(= If he doesn't write himself a note, he will forget to pay his bills.)
We told him we wouldn't come to the meeting **unless he apologized for his outburst**.
(= We told him we wouldn't come to the meeting if he didn't apologize.)

Note: You can also use the transition word Otherwise at the beginning of a sentence to express the consequences of an action or a lack of action.

He needs to write himself a note. **Otherwise**, he'll forget to pay his bills.
I always set my alarm for 7:00 A.M. on weekdays. **Otherwise**, I'm late for school.

Remember: The unreal conditional with if only expresses a wish for a particular condition (or a strong regret).
If only I were more organized, I'd get a lot more done.
(= I wish I were OR I regret that I'm not)

GRAMMAR BOOSTER p. 133
More conjunctions and transitions

DIGITAL MORE EXERCISES

D UNDERSTAND THE GRAMMAR Choose the statement with the same meaning.

1 I find it difficult to remember my appointments unless I put a reminder on my smart phone.
  a If I don't put a reminder on my smart phone, I find it difficult to remember my appointments.
  b If I don't put a reminder on my smart phone, I don't find it difficult to remember my appointments.

2 Even if she tries not to be controlling, her friends still think she is.
  a Her friends find her to be controlling, no matter what she does.
  b Her friends find her to be controlling unless she tries not to be.

3 Only if he takes a workshop about procrastination will Martin stop putting things off.
  a Unless Martin takes a workshop, he won't stop putting things off.
  b Whether or not Martin takes a workshop, he won't stop putting things off.

4 Whether or not you apologize, some people always have a hard time picking up the pieces after you tell them off.
  a It's always difficult to pick up the pieces after being told off, even if you receive an apology.
  b It's never difficult to pick up the pieces after being told off if you receive an apology.

5 You should try not to overreact when your manager criticizes your work. Otherwise, you might lose your job.
  a Unless you try to stop overreacting to your manager's criticisms, you might lose your job.
  b No matter how you react to your manager's criticisms, you might lose your job.

E GRAMMAR PRACTICE Circle the correct way to complete each statement.

1 (Whether or not / Unless) Bob is oversensitive, his friends still like him.
2 (Only if / Unless) Sal overreacts again at the meeting, I won't mention his negative attitude.
3 Katia loses her cool with her kids (only if / if only) she's had a bad day at work.
4 Carl's colleagues enjoy working with him (even if / unless) he's a bit hot-tempered.
5 (If only / Unless) she really goes overboard, I don't care that much if my wife tells me off.
6 (Only if / Even if) she puts something off to the last minute does Stacey worry about what her boss will think.

PRONUNCIATION BOOSTER p. 145
Shifting emphatic stress

NOW YOU CAN Discuss how to overcome shortcomings

A NOTEPADDING Look at page 38 again and choose three of the people's shortcomings. On your notepad, suggest how to overcome each shortcoming.

What is the shortcoming?	Your suggestions for how to overcome it
1. Ricardo is oversensitive.	try not to overreact
	remember that most people just want to be helpful

What is the shortcoming?	Your suggestions for how to overcome it
1.	
2.	
3.	

DIGITAL VIDEO

B DISCUSSION ACTIVATOR Discuss the shortcomings on your notepads and other ways you think someone could overcome them. Use adverb clauses of condition. Say as much as you can.

"Whether or not you have a good reason to be angry, you should try not to take it out on someone else."

LESSON 2 **GOAL** Acknowledge inconsiderate behavior

DIGITAL INDUCTIVE ACTIVITY

A GRAMMAR CLEFT SENTENCES: REVIEW AND EXPANSION

Cleft sentences with What

Remember: A cleft sentence emphasizes an action or a result. You can form a cleft sentence using a noun clause with What as the subject + a form of be. Be sure the form of be agrees with its complement.

What bothers me is getting interrupted when I'm speaking.
What surprised me were the many "thank you" e-mails I received.

Cleft sentences with What often have a subject complement that is a noun clause. If so, always use a singular form of be.

What bothered me the most was **(that) you didn't even apologize.**
What was surprising was **(that) she had completely cleaned up her desk.**
What I mean is **(that) I wish I hadn't lost my cool.**
What I'm trying to say is **(that) I'm really sorry.**

GRAMMAR BOOSTER p. 134
Cleft sentences: more on meaning and use

Cleft sentences with It

A cleft sentence with the impersonal It emphasizes a noun or noun phrase. Use a noun clause with who or that.

Valerie decided to have a talk with her boss. → **It was Valerie who** decided to have a talk with her boss.
Jack's outbursts make people uncomfortable. → **It's Jack's outbursts that** make people uncomfortable.

DIGITAL MORE EXERCISES

B NOTICE THE GRAMMAR

Look at Spotlight on page 39. Find and underline two types of cleft sentences in the last paragraph.

C ▶ 2:18 LISTEN TO ACTIVATE GRAMMAR

Listen to the conversations. Then listen again and complete each statement.

1 It was her ...... that he wanted to bring up.
  a missing the meeting b not finishing the project
2 What bothered him was that Simon ....
  a lost his cool b refused to apologize
3 It was his ...... that made her decide to talk with him.
  a apologizing for his mistake b interrupting her meeting
4 What's surprising to him is that the two women ....
  a are such good friends b had such a bad argument
5 It was his ...... that upset her.
  a constant criticism b refusing to listen to her

D GRAMMAR PRACTICE

Combine each pair of sentences by writing a cleft sentence with What and a noun clause subject complement.

Example: People tell me I'm too controlling. That has always surprised me.
What has always surprised me is that people tell me I'm too controlling.

1 My boss always criticizes me. That makes me kind of angry.
....

2 Most people tell lies to protect the ones they love. That fascinates me.
....

3 Gary actually has a hard time saying no to people. That's surprising.
....

4 My manager and I get along really well. That's nice.

....

5 It's been great working with you. That's what I've always wanted to tell you.

....

6 I wish you would try to control your anger. That's what I mean.

....

E **GRAMMAR PRACTICE** Write cleft sentences with It, emphasizing the underlined noun phrase.

Example: The way she talks to people is so offensive.

It's the way she talks to people that's so offensive.

1 Nancy's negative attitude prevents her from accepting any suggestions.

....

2 The final workshop can give you some ideas for getting more organized.

....

3 Bill's being so hot-tempered makes me want to avoid him.

....

4 The way you spoke to me this morning hurt my feelings.

....

5 His lying about what happened was so surprising.

....

NOW YOU CAN Acknowledge inconsiderate behavior

A 2:19 **CONVERSATION SPOTLIGHT** Read and listen. Notice the spotlighted conversation strategies.

A: Nancy, **there's something I need to bring up**.
B: Of course, Scott. What's wrong?
A: Well, the other day at the meeting, I was in the middle of making a point and you interrupted me. What really bothered me was that you didn't even let me finish my thought.
B: **I didn't realize that**! I'm so sorry. **I didn't mean to** be rude.
A: Well, I don't want to make an issue out of it, but it's been bugging me. I hope you don't mind my pointing it out.
B: **On the contrary. I can see your point**. Thanks for saying something.

B 2:20 **RHYTHM AND INTONATION** Listen again and repeat. Then practice the conversation with a partner.

DIGITAL VIDEO
DIGITAL SPEAKING BOOSTER

C **CONVERSATION ACTIVATOR** Create a similar conversation, acknowledging someone's criticism. Start like this: *There's something I need to bring up.* Be sure to change roles and then partners.

Some possible problems
being late
missing a meeting
losing one's cool
being too critical
not apologizing

DON'T STOP!
- Explain the problem in greater detail and how you felt about it.
- Offer to make up for it.
- Say as much as you can.

LESSON 3

GOAL Explain how you handle anger

DIGITAL STRATEGIES **A** ▶ 2:21 **LISTENING WARM-UP VOCABULARY EXPRESSING AND CONTROLLING ANGER**
Read and listen. Then listen again and repeat.

"I lost my temper."

- **lose one's temper**
- **have a fit**
- **hit the roof**
- **go ballistic**
- **blow one's top**

got really angry

"When I'm angry about something, I prefer to just hold it in."

hold it in / **keep it inside** avoid expressing your feelings

"When I lose my cool, I take a deep breath and try to calm down."

calm down become quieter and more relaxed

"When someone tells me off, I just let it go."

let it go / **shrug it off** decide not to be bothered by something

"Running helps me let off steam when I'm feeling angry about something."

let off steam get rid of your anger in a way that does not harm anyone; for example, by doing something active

"When I'm upset about something, venting about it with a friend usually calms me down."

vent talk with someone you trust in order to express your anger at someone else

B PERSONALIZE THE VOCABULARY Use the expressions to tell about a time when you controlled your anger or lost control of it. What do you usually do to let off steam? Is there someone in particular who you can vent to when you're angry?

DIGITAL STRATEGIES **C** ▶ 2:22 **LISTEN TO SUMMARIZE THE MAIN IDEA** Listen to the interviews. On a separate sheet of paper, write a summary in one or two sentences about the purpose of the interview.

D ▶ 2:23 **LISTEN TO INFER INFORMATION** Listen again and check the correct statements.

	Joseph would ...	Celina would ...
1 If he or she were angry with his or her boss ...	☐ make an issue out of it. ☐ say what's on his mind. ☐ hold his feelings in.	☐ let off steam. ☐ say what's on her mind. ☐ hold her feelings in.
2 If he or she were angry with a friend or colleague ...	☐ take it out on someone else. ☐ probably just shrug it off. ☐ probably lose his temper.	☐ take it out on someone else. ☐ probably just shrug it off. ☐ probably not hold it in.
3 If he or she were angry with a complete stranger ...	☐ probably let it go. ☐ probably lose his temper. ☐ take it out on someone else.	☐ probably let it go. ☐ probably say what's on her mind. ☐ take it out on someone else.

NOW YOU CAN Explain how you handle anger

A FRAME YOUR IDEAS Discuss each situation with a partner. How similar is your behavior to your partner's? Describe how you would express or control your anger. Use the Vocabulary in your discussion.

Situation	How would you handle your anger?
1 A friend arrives really late to meet you for a movie.	
2 You tell a friend something in confidence and he or she doesn't keep it a secret.	
3 A classmate or colleague says bad things about you to people you know.	
4 Someone tells you off in front of a group of other people.	
5 Another driver cuts you off while you are driving.	
6 Someone borrows something from you and doesn't return it.	
7 Your next-door neighbor always plays very loud music and has noisy late-night parties.	
8 (your own idea)	

DIGITAL SPEAKING BOOSTER

B DISCUSSION Do you act the same way when you get angry with someone you know as you do with a stranger? Explain.

OPTIONAL WRITING Write a true story about something that made you angry. What happened? How did you respond? Use the Vocabulary.

RECYCLE THIS LANGUAGE

- lose one's cool
- set someone off
- make a big issue out of something
- tell someone off
- take it out on someone
- mess up big time
- take it [well / badly]
- Even if ...
- Whether or not ...
- Only if ...
- Unless ...
- Otherwise, ...

GOAL Explore the qualities of friendship

A READING WARM-UP How do friendships among men differ from friendships among women? How are they similar?

DIGITAL STRATEGIES **B** ▶ 2:24 **READING** Read the article. Which qualities of friendship do you think are the most important?

FRIENDS THROUGH THICK AND THIN

What makes friendships stand the test of time? We interviewed 100 men and women, and here is what they had to say:

1. Friends share the good times

You build great memories together. There's nothing like having a friend around to enjoy the best moments of your life with you—graduation, your first rock concert, watching the World Cup, your wedding, and so on. You probably share a similar sense of humor and you can count on your friends to laugh at your jokes—even when they're dumb jokes. Most importantly, good friends aren't jealous of your successes. On the contrary, they cheer you on, which contributes to your achievement. Good friends want only the best for you. Otherwise, what's the point?

2. Friends are there when times are tough

Like the song says, friendship is "like a bridge over troubled water." You can always count on your friends' support when you really need a helping hand. You shouldn't even have to ask. When you're feeling down or are upset about something, friends know what makes you tick—whether or not you want to talk about it. They are thoughtful when it comes to your well-being, and they will accommodate your needs, particularly when you need it the most.

3. Friends don't judge each other

We need our friends to be dependable—through thick and thin. Your friends accept you as you are, and they don't constantly try to change you. And they roll with the punches. They get it that inside you're a good person with flaws, and that those shortcomings are part of who you are. They know you make mistakes, and they forgive you for them, knowing you'll try to do better next time. And even when someone lets you have it when you make a mistake, friends still stick up for you, because friends are patient even when you're being difficult. Even if you and your friends disagree, you respect each other's opinions.

4. Friends are trustworthy

You need your friends to be totally loyal. Above all, you need to know that your secrets are safe with them. If there's a problem between you, a friend will come to you first and not gossip about you with others. We can always count on our friends to be honest with us when others aren't. We can trust them to stick by us no matter what. Friends don't keep things bottled up inside—if there's a problem, they work things out and move on.

Are there differences between what men and women expect in their friends? Among our interviewees, husbands claimed to understand what made their wives' female friendships tick, but many wives admitted that they wondered what in the world their husbands and their male friends saw in each other. According to the women, the quality of interaction between women friends was crucial to the longevity of their friendships. They valued being able to talk about their problems and feelings. However, for the men, it was mutual acceptance—being able to simply hang out together with no judgment. One man offered this view, "Female friends prefer to face each other, while male friends do things side by side." Nevertheless, it shouldn't be all that surprising that the men and women generally agreed that *all* truly good friends stick by each other through thick and thin.

C UNDERSTAND MEANING FROM CONTEXT Find the words and expressions in the article. Use the context of the article to complete each statement.

1 When a friendship can "stand the test of time," it ...... as people change and get older.
  a continues **b** becomes more difficult

2 When you "count on people" to do something, you ....
  a worry whether they will do it **b** feel sure they will do it

3 When someone "cheers you on," he or she is ...... of your efforts.
  a supportive **b** critical

4 When "times are tough," things are ....
  a going well **b** difficult

5 When you know what "makes someone tick," you understand ....
  a how he or she thinks and responds to things **b** that he or she likes you

6 When people are friends "through thick and thin," their friendship ....
  a can survive good times and bad times **b** may be in trouble

7 When someone "lets you have it," he or she ....
  a is being very critical **b** is being very supportive

8 When someone "sticks up for you," he or she ....
a defends you against criticism
b criticizes you honestly

9 When friends "stick by you," they ....
a are always loyal to you
b tell you off

10 When someone "keeps things bottled up inside," he or she ...... to talk about uncomfortable feelings such as anger.
a is willing
b isn't willing

D **APPLY IDEAS** Discuss what a good friend would do in response to each situation, waccording to the information in the article. Explain your answers.

1 You get a new job at twice your current salary.

> "It says a true friend cheers you on when times are good. So I think a good friend would be happy for me and want to celebrate."

2 You tell your friend a really dumb joke.

3 You're unhappy about something, but you haven't told anyone about it yet.

4 You lose your temper with your friend.

5 A colleague criticizes you when you're not around.

6 You and your friend have a disagreement.

E **RELATE TO PERSONAL EXPERIENCE** Work in pairs. Using the four qualities of a good friendship in the article as examples, share personal examples of your friendships that illustrate each quality.

DIGITAL EXTRA CHALLENGE

NOW YOU CAN Explore the qualities of friendship

A **FRAME YOUR IDEAS** Read each statement and write A, B, or C. Then, with a partner, compare and explain your responses.

> "That's not the kind of friend I am. Remember what the article said? Good friends aren't jealous of your successes."

A = That's not the kind of friend I am.
B = Sometimes I'm a bit like that.
C = I have to admit that sounds a lot like me.

"My friend Carla just got engaged last week. I can't figure it out. I'm so much more popular than she is." ☐

"My friend Trevor is really feeling down right now because he split up with his girlfriend. He's kind of getting on my nerves. I wish he'd just stop talking about it." ☐

"Laura's a good friend, but I think her clothes are really out of style. It's kind of embarrassing to be seen with her. She'd be so much prettier if she took my suggestions." ☐

"I was really disappointed when my friend Tom didn't invite me over to watch the World Cup. I guess I just won't invite him anywhere either." ☐

"My friend Harriet told me about the problems she's been having with her husband. I only told my neighbor Cynthia about it, but no one else." ☐

"My friend Nick is always late for everything. Today was the last straw—if he can't change his habits, he can go find *another* friend." ☐

B **DISCUSSION** How would you rate your friendships in general? All things considered, in what ways would you say you're a good friend to *your* friends? Explain your answers and give examples.

How I'd generally rate my friends

poor — average — excellent

How I'd rate myself as a friend

poor — average — excellent

WRITING Transitional topic sentences

A WRITING SKILL Study the rules.

Remember: Transition words and subordinating conjunctions link ideas within and between sentences.

They can also be used in a paragraph's topic sentence to connect the paragraph to the one that precedes it.

The following words and phrases can be used as transitions to announce the content of a new paragraph:

To add information

Furthermore, it's very convenient.

Moreover, it's very convenient.

More importantly, it's very convenient.

To contrast information

Even though it's convenient, it's not for everyone.

Although it's convenient, it's not for everyone.

Despite the fact that it's convenient, it's not for everyone.

Nevertheless, it's not for everyone.

On the other hand, it's not for everyone.

However, it's not for everyone.

WRITING MODEL

For an effective solution to procrastination, I suggest using the daily calendar on your smartphone. It can be used to break up the steps essential to completing a larger task into smaller tasks. That way it is easier to keep things moving forward. It also allows you to check off the smaller tasks as they are finished, which motivates you by providing a feeling of accomplishment.

Furthermore, using a smartphone calendar is not really all that difficult. You can use the calendar that's already installed, or you can download an app for that purpose. Instructions are easily available online, and they are usually very clear.

Nevertheless, using a smartphone calendar does take some getting used to. It may require some time to learn how to use it, but the calendar will make your work easier. Without a calendar, it is far too easy to simply forget about what needs to be done. With one, it is easy to keep track of your progress. If your teacher or manager asks questions, you have a record you can refer to. This increases your confidence. I believe the calendar is one of the best ways to convert procrastination into effective organization.

B PRACTICE Rewrite these transitional topic sentences from the Writing Model, using other words and phrases to announce the content of the new paragraph. (Note: You may have to make other changes in the sentence.)

Furthermore, using a smartphone calendar is not really all that difficult.

1 More importantly, ...

2 Moreover, ...

Nevertheless, using a smartphone calendar does take some getting used to.

3 Even though ....

4 Although ....

5 Despite the fact that ....

6 On the other hand, ...

7 However, ...

DIGITAL WRITING PROCESS

C APPLY THE WRITING SKILL Write a three-paragraph essay presenting a solution to a common shortcoming. In paragraph one, introduce the solution. Use transitional topic sentences to link the content of the second and third paragraphs.

SELF-CHECK

- ☐ Does the first paragraph have a topic sentence?
- ☐ Do the paragraphs that follow have transitional topic sentences?
- ☐ Does each transitional topic sentence clearly link to previous content?

DIGITAL GAME

REVIEW

A ▶ 2:25 **Listen to three people describe their shortcomings. Then listen again and complete the chart. Listen a third time if necessary to check your answers.**

	What is the shortcoming?	What solution did the person find?	Did it work?
1			
2			
3			

B **Complete each statement with one of the lettered choices. (You will not use all the choices.)**

1 Claire overreacts and takes things personally when her friends make suggestions. She ....
2 Bob is always losing his cool over things that aren't important. He ....
3 Laura usually misses her deadlines because she doesn't get started on her assignments right away. She ....
4 Nick is always worrying about every little detail. He hates making mistakes. He ....

a is a perfectionist.
b is negative.
c tends to procrastinate.
d is oversensitive.
e is hot-tempered.

C **Complete each statement about the situations in which people express or control their anger.**

1 People sometimes hold their feelings in when ....
....
2 People usually only tell someone off when ....
....
3 Most people lose their tempers only when ....
....

D **Complete each statement logically and correctly with one of the lettered choices.**

1 Even if I know a project is important, ...
2 Unless I know that a project is not important, ...
3 Only if I know that a project is not important ....
4 If only I had known that the project was important, ...
5 I wish I'd known that the project was so important. ......

a Otherwise, I wouldn't have waited till the last minute to get started.
b I never wait till the last minute to get started.
c will I wait till the last minute to get started.
d I still wait till the last minute to get started.
e I wouldn't have waited till the last minute to get started.

E **On a separate sheet of paper, rewrite each sentence as a cleft sentence with What. Follow the example.**

1 It's the way she criticizes new employees that's so offensive.

What's so offensive is the way she criticizes new employees.

2 It's maintaining a positive attitude that changes negative thinking.
3 It's fear of failure that causes people to put things off.
4 It's his being so hot-tempered that makes people feel like they're walking on eggshells.
5 It's her ability to organize that makes her so successful.

TEST-TAKING SKILLS BOOSTER p. 154

Web Project: Anger Management
www.english.com/summit3e

UNIT
5 Humor

COMMUNICATION GOALS
1 Discuss the health benefits of laughter
2 Respond to something funny
3 Analyze what makes us laugh
4 Explore the limits of humor

PREVIEW

A FRAME YOUR IDEAS Take the humor self-test to analyze your sense of humor.

B PAIR WORK Discuss your funniest and least funny choices with a partner. Explain why you find some of the images funny and other ones not funny. Do you have the same sense of humor?

> "I don't like the picture of the boy with the head to his side. I find it kind of scary—even a bit creepy. I gave it a 1."

C DISCUSSION Do a class survey. Which image did your classmates find the funniest? Which did they find the least funny? What were the reasons?

ENGLISH FOR TODAY'S WORLD
Understand a variety of accents.
Sylvie = French
David = American English (standard)

D ▶ 3:02 **SPOTLIGHT** Read and listen to a conversation about an embarrassing social situation. Notice the spotlighted language.

Sylvie: Oh, David, I can't tell you how mortified I am.
David: What on earth happened?
Sylvie: So, last night I told this funny joke French people tell about Americans: How do you know someone's an American? He asks for ketchup for his peanut butter sandwich. Well, **it went over like a lead balloon**. *No one laughed*. **I made a total fool of myself**.
David: Oh, Sylvie! That must have been awful!
Sylvie: The thing is I don't know why they took it personally. The joke wasn't about *them*! They were pretty sophisticated. We were even eating French food!
David: Well, you couldn't have known this, but it's definitely uncool to make fun of a particular nationality, an ethnic group, a religion … **It just isn't done**.
Sylvie: You mean you guys are that politically correct?
David: You could say that. And the fact that you're French probably didn't help. We Americans can get a bit intimidated by the French, but don't quote me on that.
Sylvie: **I don't get it**. Why are people here so sensitive? In France, we can't get enough jokes about ourselves.
David: I'm surmising the French are thicker-skinned than Americans …
Sylvie: You can say that again. Ethnic jokes—even ones about ourselves—are just **par for the course** there. You know, I don't think I can ever face those people again.
David: You know what, Sylvie? We Americans make jokes about ourselves, too. It's just less funny when it comes from an outsider. **Don't take it so hard.**
Sylvie: **Easier said than done!**

E **UNDERSTAND IDIOMS AND EXPRESSIONS** Complete the statements with spotlighted language.

1 If you want to say that someone's advice isn't easy to follow, you can say " ...."
2 Another way to say that no one liked your joke is " ...."
3 When you want to say you just don't understand something, you can say " ...."
4 When you want to suggest that something isn't at all unusual, you can say it's " ...."
5 When you want to suggest that most people consider something rude or inappropriate, you can say " ...."
6 If you do something stupid or silly that causes other people to laugh at you, you feel embarrassed and say " ...."
7 If you want to suggest that someone is reacting too strongly to something, you can tell him or her " ...."

F **THINK AND EXPLAIN** Can a joke about your own nationality or ethnic group ever be funny? Or are those jokes always "politically incorrect" or even offensive? Explain.

SPEAKING **PAIR WORK** Check the things you find funny. Discuss why certain things make people laugh. What other things make you laugh?

☐ Cute video clips about animals and babies	☐ People embarrassing themselves by using the wrong word or expression
☐ Physical "slapstick" humor in TV shows and movies	☐ Stories or pictures of people making fools of themselves
☐ Jokes making fun of men or jokes making fun of women	☐ Your own idea:

"Even though some ethnic jokes can be funny, I think we probably shouldn't tell them. They can end up insulting people."

LESSON 1

GOAL Discuss the health benefits of laughter

A laughter therapy group

A ▶ 3:03 **GRAMMAR SPOTLIGHT** Read the article about the health benefits of laughter. Notice the spotlighted grammar.

LAUGH YOUR WAY TO HEALTH?

CAN SOMETHING AS SIMPLE AS LAUGHTER CURE DISEASE?

The concept is actually not new. Sixteenth-century humanist educator Richard Mulcaster **said** that because laughter **produced** warmth in the body, it **might be** a good remedy for colds. Other scientists of his time **noted** that laughter **increased** the rate of breathing, **boosted** muscle tone, and **exercised** the body's internal organs. They **claimed** that those effects **were** beneficial to people suffering from colds too. So although many physicians and medical researchers had long **thought** that laughter **could be** helpful, scientific studies had been inconclusive. Then, in his classic 1956 book *The Stress of Life*, Hungarian scientist Hans Selye **wrote**, based on extensive research, that he **had proved** that biological stress **has** negative effects on health. This laid the foundation for the theory that the absence of stress could have positive effects.

Later, in 1976, American editor Norman Cousins—a non-scientist—**reported** in the *New England Journal of Medicine* that laughter **had helped** cure him of a painful life-threatening chronic disease. His article captured the attention of the medical profession and some doctors began considering using laughter as therapy. Then in his 1979 bestseller, *Anatomy of an Illness*, Cousins **wrote** that he **had been** so sick that the only thing he could do was lie in bed. Cousins **theorized** that, based on Selye's research, because the stress of negative emotions **could cause** illness, positive emotions **should be able to exert** a healing effect. So he spent his time watching funny movies and he asked his friends to tell him lots of funny jokes.

Although no one **can state** definitively that laughter **cured** Norman Cousins, the concept of laughter therapy has gained popular acceptance, notably in Madan Kataria's laughter yoga movement practiced by thousands of people worldwide. In this popular activity, large groups of people sit together and force themselves to laugh until the laughter becomes contagious and real.

B **CRITICAL THINKING** Do you think it's possible that Norman Cousins was cured by laughter? Can you think of any other explanation for his recovery? In what ways do you think positive and negative emotions can affect our health?

DIGITAL INDUCTIVE ACTIVITY

C **GRAMMAR** **INDIRECT SPEECH: BACKSHIFTS IN TENSE AND TIME EXPRESSIONS**

In indirect speech, when the reporting verb is in a past form, the verb form in the noun clause (the indirect speech) usually "shifts back" to preserve meaning. Compare the verb forms in direct and indirect speech.

Some common reporting verbs

admit	insist	theorize
claim	note	think
complain	report	write
continue	state	

Direct speech	Indirect speech
Dr. Ames wrote, "Negative emotions **are** harmful and **cause** illness."	Dr. Ames wrote (that) negative emotions **were** harmful and **caused** illness.
He continued, "But Cousins **hasn't proved** anything."	He continued (that) Cousins **hadn't proved** anything.
Cousins said, "Laughter **cured** me."	Cousins said (that) laughter **had cured** him.
We wrote, "He **isn't practicing** laughter yoga."	We wrote (that) he **wasn't practicing** laughter yoga.
She claimed, "We **were telling** the truth."	She claimed (that) they **had been telling** the truth.
Doctors admitted, "We**'ve learned** from Cousins's article.	Doctors admitted (that) they **had learned** from Cousins's article.
He told her, "I**'ll check** to see how you**'re feeling** later."	He told her (that) he **would check** to see how she **was feeling** later.
Pam told us, "I **can't understand** what **happened**."	Pam told us (that) she **couldn't understand** what **had happened**.
He told me, "You **have to see** this funny movie."	He told me (that) I **had to see** that funny movie.
The nurse told the little girl, "You **must rest**."	The nurse told the little girl (that) she **had to rest**.

Exceptions

When a reporting verb is in the simple past tense, backshifting is optional when the statement refers to something just said, something that's still true, or a scientific or general truth.

Tom just called. He said that the director **is** (OR **was**) leaving. [something just said]

Ann told me that she **needs** (OR **needed**) to renew her passport. [something still true]

He noted that the Earth **is** (OR **was**) the fifth largest planet in the solar system. [a scientific or general truth]

Do not make changes to present or perfect forms of the modals should, could, may, might, would, and ought to when converting to indirect speech.

Expressions of time and place: backshifts in indirect speech

now →	**then**	this year →	**that year**
today →	**that day**	last week →	**the week before**
tomorrow →	**the next day**	next month →	**the following month**
yesterday →	**the day before**	here →	**there**

Mark told me, "Judy was here yesterday." → Mark told me Judy had been **there the day before.**

GRAMMAR BOOSTER p. 135

Indirect speech: review and expansion
- Imperatives in indirect speech
- Changes to pronouns and possessives
- Say, tell, and ask
- Other reporting verbs

DIGITAL MORE EXERCISES

D GRAMMAR PRACTICE On a separate sheet of paper, rewrite the sentences in indirect speech. If the sentence can be written both with and without backshifting, write it both ways.

1 Ms. Barr stated, "I want you to finish your essays for the next class."
2 Last week I told my husband, "This has been the best vacation we've ever taken."
3 My friend Amy said, "I have never seen such exciting paintings before."
4 In his lecture, Dr. White explained, "The earth rotates around the sun."

E PAIR WORK With a partner, take turns restating each of the following in indirect speech.

1 Pain researchers reported, "Laughter may help some patients."
2 They said, "Our new study will begin here next week."
3 The doctors said, "We've recommended laughter yoga to cure his pain."
4 The patient told everyone, "I definitely feel better from the laughter yoga."

F GRAMMAR PRACTICE On a separate sheet of paper, write what the people actually said, using direct speech.

1 Ellen told me she had read an article about laughter yoga in the New Yorker magazine.
2 She claimed she believed laughter yoga could be helpful.
3 I said I never would have known that.
4 The nurse told me that she had been using laughter therapy with certain patients.

NOW YOU CAN Discuss the health benefits of laughter

A NOTEPADDING Complete the statements, based on the article. Then use that information as support in the Discussion Activator.

Richard Mulcaster and other scientists have said that

Much later, Hans Selye wrote that

Norman Cousins claimed that

DIGITAL VIDEO

B DISCUSSION ACTIVATOR Do you believe laughter can be "good medicine"? How could you apply the ideas in the article to help heal a sick friend or family member? If you were very sick, how might you use laughter therapy to get better? Support your opinion with ideas from the article, using indirect speech if you are reporting what someone said. Say as much as you can.

LESSON 2

GOAL Respond to something funny

A ▶ 3:04 **VOCABULARY** **WAYS TO RESPOND TO JOKES AND OTHER FUNNY THINGS**
Read and listen. Then listen again and repeat.

ALSO: That's ridiculous / silly / offensive*

* Be careful! These can be rude and hurt the joke-teller's feelings.

B ▶ 3:05 **LISTEN TO ACTIVATE VOCABULARY** Listen to six conversations. After each one, check Yes or No to indicate whether the listener thought it was funny. Then listen again and write your *own* response to each joke, using the Vocabulary.

Did the listener think it was funny?

	Yes	No	Your *own* response to the joke
1	☐	☐	....
2	☐	☐	....
3	☐	☐	....
4	☐	☐	....
5	☐	☐	....
6	☐	☐	....

C **PAIR WORK** Did you both get all the jokes? If there's a joke your partner didn't get (or didn't like), try to explain why it was funny to you. Tell your partner which joke you thought was the funniest, and why.

D **RELATE TO PERSONAL EXPERIENCE** Tell your partner about something funny you saw on TV or in a movie, or a joke or funny story you heard from a friend or family member. Respond to your partner, using the Vocabulary.

DIGITAL INDUCTIVE ACTIVITY

E **GRAMMAR** **QUESTIONS IN INDIRECT SPEECH**

Indirect questions are a kind of embedded question—a question that is included in a noun clause.
Indirect yes / no questions begin with if or whether (or whether or not).

He asked, "Did you find that joke funny?" → He asked **if I had found the joke funny.** OR He asked **whether or not I had found the joke funny.**

My boss asked me, "Were you able to finish the project yesterday?" → My boss asked **if** (or **whether**) **I had been able to finish the project the day before.**

Indirect information questions begin with a question word.

She asked, "How did you respond to that offensive joke?" → She asked **how I had responded to that offensive joke.**

People often ask Nora, "How many years have you been studying English?" → People often ask Nora **how many years she has been studying English.**

Remember: Embedded questions always have statement (not inverted) word order. Do not use do, does, or did.
My friend asked what movie I wanted to see. NOT My friend asked what movie ~~did I want~~ to see.

DIGITAL MORE EXERCISES

F **GRAMMAR PRACTICE** On a separate sheet of paper, rewrite each sentence in indirect speech. Make all necessary backshifts and changes to pronouns and time expressions.

1 The teacher asked her students, "Can you tell me what the joke is about?"
2 Barry sometimes asks himself, "How would I react if someone told an offensive joke?"
3 Lisa asked her boyfriend, "Should you have laughed at that offensive joke?"
4 Dan asked his wife, "Have you finished reading that book of jokes?"
5 Vivian asked me, "Which is the best website for funny animal videos?"

PRONUNCIATION BOOSTER p. 146
Intonation of sarcasm

NOW YOU CAN Respond to something funny

A ▶ 3:06 **CONVERSATION SPOTLIGHT** Read and listen. Notice the spotlighted conversation strategies.

A: Oh, Melanie, **you've got to see this**! I just can't tell you how hilarious it is.
B: What is it?
A: Here. It's this video. Some guy keeps tearing pieces of paper and his baby's laughing hysterically. **Seriously**, come over here and look!
B: Oh, **that's priceless**! Forward me the link, OK?
A: **Totally**.

B ▶ 3:07 **RHYTHM AND INTONATION** Listen again and repeat. Then practice the conversation with a partner.

DIGITAL VIDEO
DIGITAL SPEAKING BOOSTER

C **CONVERSATION ACTIVATOR** Bring a cartoon, photo, or video clip to class. Or use the cartoon below or something from page 50. Use it to create a similar conversation. Start like this: *You've got to see this …* Be sure to change roles and then partners.

DON'T STOP!

- Talk about other cartoons, videos, or video clips you've seen.
- Say why you think they're funny.
- Say as much as you can.

"It could be that it's not plugged in, but that would be too easy."

LESSON 3 **GOAL** Analyze what makes us laugh

A READING WARM-UP Who are your favorite comedians and comic actors? Why do they make you laugh?

DIGITAL STRATEGIES **B** ▶ 3:08 **READING** Read the article about why people laugh. Provide your own examples to illustrate each theory.

THEORIES OF HUMOR

People of all ages and from all cultures laugh. Although there are many factors that make something funny, three theories are often cited.

THE SUPERIORITY THEORY

The Superiority Theory holds that we tend to find people's small misfortunes and verbal or behavioral mistakes funny. Two examples of the kind of misfortunes often depicted in funny movies and comedy routines are people falling down or bumping into things. Similarly, hearing someone mispronounce a word or use the wrong word makes us laugh, as do the ridiculous mistakes that result from automatic spell check programs. According to this theory, the reason why we laugh at the misfortunes or mistakes of others is that they make us feel superior (and happy that the mistakes and misfortunes are theirs, not ours!).

THE INCONGRUITY THEORY

The Incongruity Theory suggests that humor arises from unexpected, inappropriate, or illogical situations—such as the one about the man who says his brother thinks he's a chicken:

> A man goes to a psychiatrist and says, "Doctor, I'm worried about my brother. He thinks he's a chicken." "That IS serious," says the doctor. "Why don't you put him in a mental hospital?" So the man says, "I would, but I need the eggs."

According to the Incongruity Theory, a joke becomes funny when we anticipate that one thing will happen or be said, but something else does instead. When the joke goes in the unexpected direction, we experience two sets of incompatible thoughts and emotions—the ones we had as we were listening and the ones revealed at the end. This incongruity makes us laugh.

THE RELIEF THEORY

According to the Relief Theory, humor is the feeling of relief that comes from the removal of tension. When tension is high, we need a release, and laughter is a way to cleanse our system of the built-up tension. This theory holds that there are certain things we feel tense about, such as bodily functions, physical attractions, and shame about how we look. It is believed that the large number of jokes about those subjects come from our need to laugh about them and thus relieve or reduce our tension about them.

Regardless of the theory, in order to be able to appreciate a situation or joke as funny, some detachment is always necessary; that is, we have to feel uninvolved with the situation. For example, we can often laugh at our own past mistakes because, with the passage of time, we have become detached. Conversely, if the joke or situation is too familiar or realistic, it may "hit too close to home" and evoke sadness instead of laughter. To understand a joke—to "get it"—we might also need some knowledge of cultural, economic, political, and social issues, without which some jokes are impossible to understand. Although humor is universal, there is no universal joke.

C CLASSIFY Complete the chart, checking the theory you think best explains why people laugh. (You may choose more than one.) Explain your choices.

PEOPLE OFTEN LAUGH WHEN THEY ...	THE SUPERIORITY THEORY	THE INCONGRUITY THEORY	THE RELIEF THEORY
discover the strange noise they heard downstairs was only the cat.	☐	☐	☐
see someone slip and fall down.	☐	☐	☐
see someone wearing inappropriate clothes to an event.	☐	☐	☐
arrive at a party where someone is wearing the same outfit.	☐	☐	☐
see a little girl wearing her mother's high heels.	☐	☐	☐
see someone make an embarrassing social mistake.	☐	☐	☐

D ▶ 3:09 **LISTEN TO APPLY IDEAS** Listen to three jokes. Write the theory you think each joke exemplifies. Then discuss with a partner to see if you agreed or disagreed. Provide reasons for your opinion and listen again if necessary to settle differences of opinion.

DIGITAL EXTRA CHALLENGE

NOW YOU CAN Analyze what makes us laugh

DIGITAL SPEAKING BOOSTER

DISCUSSION Read the list of common types of jokes to the right and try to explain why people find each kind funny. Use the theories, other reasons, and your own ideas for support.

OPTIONAL WRITING On a separate sheet of paper, write a joke you like. Then write at least two paragraphs analyzing why you and other people find it funny.

DIGITAL STRATEGIES

▶ 3:10 **Common types of jokes**

a dirty joke	a joke about sex or with sexual content
an ethnic joke	a joke about people of a particular ethnic background
a sexist joke	a joke about men or women
a political joke	a joke about a political candidate, party, opinion, or government official
a verbal joke	a joke that uses language in such a way that the language itself becomes funny

GOAL Explore the limits of humor

DIGITAL STRATEGIES **A** ▶ 3:11 **LISTENING WARM-UP VOCABULARY PRACTICAL JOKES**
Read and listen. Then listen again and repeat.

be the butt of a joke be the person on whom a trick, or "practical joke," is played; be the object of ridicule

can take a joke / be a good sport be able to laugh at a practical joke, even when one is the butt of it, without getting insulted or taking it too personally

be in bad (or **poor**) **taste** be offensive or extremely cruel

cross the line go beyond funny into something mean, hurtful, offensive, or cruel

DIGITAL STRATEGIES **B** ▶ 3:12 **LISTEN TO ACTIVATE VOCABULARY** Listen to a description of a practical joke a doctor played on another doctor. Complete each statement about the practical joke you heard described.

1 Dr. Adams ....
  a played a practical joke on another doctor
  b was the butt of another doctor's joke

2 The woman thinks her father's joke ....
  a was in pretty good taste
  b may have crossed the line

3 In the end, the younger doctor proved that ....
  a he could take being the butt of a practical joke
  b the joke was in pretty poor taste

4 We can conclude that the man thinks that ....
  a the joke crossed the line
  b the younger doctor was a pretty good sport

C ▶ 3:13 **LISTEN TO SUMMARIZE** Listen again and write a summary of the story, using indirect speech. Then compare summaries with a partner. Use the example as a way to start:

"The woman described a practical joke her father had once played on someone. One day ..."

D ▶ 3:14 **LISTEN TO TAKE NOTES** Listen to people who were the butt of practical jokes. Then listen again to complete the chart. Use the Vocabulary. Listen again if necessary.

Speaker	What was the joke?	How did the person react?
1		
2		
3		

E **DISCUSSION** Which, if any, of the jokes in Exercise D crossed the line? Explain your opinion. Then compare how you would have reacted with the way each speaker reacted.

NOW YOU CAN Explore the limits of humor

A FRAME YOUR IDEAS Read the practical jokes and rate each one, using the scorecard.

SCORECARD

X = I don't get it.
1 = It crosses the line.
2 = It's silly.
3 = It's kind of funny.
4 = It's hilarious!

A RATING: ☐

Someone in your family leaves a very real-looking toy snake in a drawer with your clothes. You open the drawer and are about to put your hand in when you suddenly see the snake.

B RATING: ☐

You start getting lots of calls from people who want to buy your house, even though you have no intention of selling. It turns out a friend had secretly created an online real estate ad offering your house at a very cheap price.

C RATING: ☐

A colleague tells you that another colleague is going to get married. When you see her, you congratulate her happily. She has no idea what you're talking about.

D RATING: ☐

Someone in your family offers you a cup of coffee or tea. When you take the first sip, it tastes so bad you can hardly swallow it. You realize it has salt in it instead of sugar.

E RATING: ☐

You're invited to a friend's costume party. When you arrive at the party, everyone is nicely dressed in regular clothes, and you are dressed in a chicken costume.

B PAIR WORK Compare your ratings on the practical jokes. Do you agree? Then, for each joke, compare how you would have responded if you had been the butt of the joke. Would you have been a good sport? Or would you have been offended?

RECYCLE THIS LANGUAGE

- It was so [hysterical / hilarious]!
- It was [too much / too funny]!
- I didn't get it.
- What was so funny about it?
- It went over my head.
- Seriously.
- That just isn't done.
- It was kind of [ridiculous / offensive / silly].

C DISCUSSION

1 When do you think a practical joke crosses the line?
2 Have you ever played a practical joke on someone else? What was the joke and what happened? Use the Vocabulary from page 58.
3 What is your opinion of practical jokes in the workplace? Are they ever acceptable? Explain.

WRITING Writing dialogue

A WRITING SKILL Study the rules.

Paragraphing a story with dialogue
With direct speech, begin a new paragraph each time you introduce a new speaker. Remember that paragraphs should be indented or should have a space above them so the reader can see where new paragraphs begin. See one paragraphing style in the Writing Model.

Punctuation of direct speech

- When the reporting verb comes before a quotation, put a comma after the reporting verb. Put the end punctuation inside the quotation marks.

  Mr. Mann said, "That's not at all funny."

- When the reporting verb comes after a quotation, put a comma, question mark, or an exclamation point at the end of the quoted sentence, inside the quotation marks. Put the speaker's name before or after the reporting verb.

  "Please don't do anything cruel," Ms. Kane said.
  "Didn't anyone object to that mean practical joke?" asked Carlson.

- A reporting verb can also come between two parts of a quotation. Put quotation marks around each part of the quotation. Don't begin the second part of the quotation with a capital letter unless it begins a new sentence.

  "Melanie and Elaine," Mr. Sargent said, "please apologize for hurting Morgan."

- If the reporting verb comes between complete sentences, put a period after the reporting verb. Begin the new sentence with a capital letter.

  "Peter, please apologize to Morgan," continued Mr. Sargent. "You participated in that mean practical joke too."

WRITING MODEL

About a year ago, my grandmother was walking down the street, stopping from time to time to look in shop windows. At one store, she stopped to admire a dress in the window. Just as she turned to enter the store, a businessman walking very fast and, not looking where he was going, bumped into her, knocking her down.

"Oh, I'm so sorry!" said the man. "Are you OK?"

My grandmother was too stunned to reply. But then after a moment she said she was fine.

"Look!" she heard someone say from across the street. "An old woman just fell down!"

She quickly sat up and looked around with great concern and said, "Where?"

When she told us this story, we all laughed. But, it really wasn't that funny, and it could have been serious.

B PRACTICE On a separate sheet of paper, rewrite the sentences, correcting the errors in punctuation and capitalization.

1 Norman Cousins said, "That he had cured himself with laughter."
2 "The Superiority Theory" our professor explained. "Is exemplified by finding people's errors funny."
3 "The joke was really cruel," said Claire. "they shouldn't have played it."
4 "Does that example illustrate the Incongruity Theory" asked John?
5 "I learned about all kinds of humor in my psychology class", said my sister.

C PRACTICE On a separate sheet of paper, write the following indirect speech statements in direct speech, using correct punctuation for dialogue.

1 Dr. Summers stated that positive emotions can have a direct effect on emotional and physical health.
2 A psychologist told me many people believed that Norman Cousins's book popularized the idea that laughter therapy could be helpful in treating illness.
3 She said that practical jokes come from our need to feel superior to others.
4 Ms. Barton insisted that traditional medicine is more effective than laughter therapy.
5 Our professor asked whether there is any scientific evidence that laughter can treat illness.

DIGITAL WRITING PROCESS

D APPLY THE WRITING SKILL Write a true or imaginary story telling what happened and what people said, using dialogue. Use the Writing Model for support.

SELF-CHECK

- ☐ Did I use direct speech in my story?
- ☐ Did I punctuate direct speech correctly?
- ☐ Did I correctly paragraph the dialogue?

DIGITAL GAME

REVIEW

A ▶ 3:15 **Listen to three examples of jokes. After each one, complete the statement about it. Listen again if necessary.**

1 The butt of the joke is ....

a John b the manager c Mark

2 The joke is funny because ....

a we feel superior to the man b we are surprised at his response c we feel relief from tension

3 This joke is an example of ....

a a verbal joke b an ethnic joke c a dirty joke

B **Write the response you would give in each situation, using vocabulary from Unit 5 or your own response.**

1 Someone tells you a joke you don't understand.

You: ....

....

2 Someone tells an insulting ethnic joke and you want to say something about it.

You: ....

....

3 You hear a joke that you find very funny.

You: ....

....

4 You have a friend who wants to play a practical joke on someone, but you think it's cruel.

You: ....

....

C **On a separate sheet of paper, rewrite the following, changing the direct speech into indirect speech.**

1 Mary asked me, "Did you get that joke?"

2 The students insisted, "We didn't play any practical jokes in the gym."

3 My father admitted, "Twenty-five years of practicing medicine have taught me that laughter can be the best medicine."

4 Jess told her friends, "I'll tell you about a joke I told during my job interview yesterday if you promise not to tell anyone."

5 "I can't understand British humor," said Anne.

6 She said, "I may not have enough familiarity with British culture to understand all the pop culture references."

7 The people at the party asked, "Who's going to tell the first joke?"

D **Complete each statement about kinds of jokes.**

1 A(n) .... joke is a joke that's about sex.

2 A joke that's insulting to all men or to all women is a(n) .... joke.

3 A joke that's insulting to all people of a certain nationality is a(n) .... joke.

4 A joke that makes fun of a candidate for election is a(n) .... joke.

5 A joke that plays a trick on someone to make him or her the butt of the joke is a(n) .... joke.

TEST-TAKING SKILLS BOOSTER p. 155

Web Project: Laughter Therapy
www.english.com/summit3e

Reference Charts

IRREGULAR VERBS

base form	simple past	past participle
be	was / were	been
beat	beat	beaten
become	became	become
begin	began	begun
bend	bent	bent
bet	bet	bet
bite	bit	bitten
bleed	bled	bled
blow	blew	blown
break	broke	broken
breed	bred	bred
bring	brought	brought
build	built	built
burn	burned / burnt	burned / burnt
burst	burst	burst
buy	bought	bought
catch	caught	caught
choose	chose	chosen
come	came	come
cost	cost	cost
creep	crept	crept
cut	cut	cut
deal	dealt	dealt
dig	dug	dug
do	did	done
draw	drew	drawn
dream	dreamed / dreamt	dreamed / dreamt
drink	drank	drunk
drive	drove	driven
eat	ate	eaten
fall	fell	fallen
feed	fed	fed
feel	felt	felt
fight	fought	fought
find	found	found
fit	fit	fit
fly	flew	flown
forbid	forbade	forbidden
forget	forgot	forgotten
forgive	forgave	forgiven
freeze	froze	frozen
get	got	gotten
give	gave	given
go	went	gone
grow	grew	grown
hang	hung	hung
have	had	had
hear	heard	heard
hide	hid	hidden
hit	hit	hit
hold	held	held
hurt	hurt	hurt
keep	kept	kept
know	knew	known
lay	laid	laid
lead	led	led
leap	leaped / leapt	leaped / leapt
learn	learned / learnt	learned / learnt
leave	left	left
lend	lent	lent
let	let	let
lie	lay	lain
light	lit	lit
lose	lost	lost
make	made	made

base form	simple past	past participle
mean	meant	meant
meet	met	met
mistake	mistook	mistaken
pay	paid	paid
put	put	put
quit	quit	quit
read /rid/	read /rɛd/	read /rɛd/
ride	rode	ridden
ring	rang	rung
rise	rose	risen
run	ran	run
say	said	said
see	saw	seen
sell	sold	sold
send	sent	sent
set	set	set
shake	shook	shaken
shed	shed	shed
shine	shone	shone
shoot	shot	shot
show	showed	shown
shrink	shrank	shrunk
shut	shut	shut
sing	sang	sung
sink	sank	sunk
sit	sat	sat
sleep	slept	slept
slide	slid	slid
smell	smelled / smelt	smelled / smelt
speak	spoke	spoken
speed	sped / speeded	sped / speeded
spell	spelled / spelt	spelled / spelt
spend	spent	spent
spill	spilled / spilt	spilled / spilt
spin	spun	spun
spit	spit / spat	spit / spat
spoil	spoiled / spoilt	spoiled / spoilt
spread	spread	spread
spring	sprang / sprung	sprang / sprung
stand	stood	stood
steal	stole	stolen
stick	stuck	stuck
sting	stung	stung
stink	stank / stunk	stunk
strike	struck	struck / stricken
string	strung	strung
swear	swore	sworn
sweep	swept	swept
swim	swam	swum
swing	swung	swung
take	took	taken
teach	taught	taught
tear	tore	torn
tell	told	told
think	thought	thought
throw	threw	thrown
understand	understood	understood
upset	upset	upset
wake	woke / waked	woken / waked
wear	wore	worn
weave	wove	woven
weep	wept	wept
win	won	won
wind	wound	wound
write	wrote	written

VERBS FOLLOWED BY A GERUND

acknowledge	celebrate	discontinue	escape	imagine	postpone	recall	risk
admit	complete	discuss	explain	justify	practice	recommend	suggest
advise	consider	dislike	feel like	keep	prevent	report	support
appreciate	delay	don't mind	finish	mention	prohibit	resent	tolerate
avoid	deny	endure	forgive	mind	propose	resist	undestand
can't help	detest	enjoy	give up	miss	quit		

EXPRESSIONS THAT CAN BE FOLLOWED BY A GERUND

be excited about	be committed to	make an excuse for	look forward to
be worried about	be opposed to	have a reason for	blame [someone or something] for
be responsible for	be used to	believe in	forgive [someone or something] for
be interested in	complain about	participate in	thank [someone or something] for
be accused of	dream about / of	succeed in	keep [someone or something] from
be capable of	talk about / of	take advantage of	prevent [someone or something] from
be tired of	think about / of	take care of	stop [someone or something] from
be accustomed to	apologize for	insist on	

VERBS FOLLOWED DIRECTLY BY AN INFINITIVE

afford	can't wait	demand	hope	need	pretend	swear	want
agree	care	deserve	hurry	neglect	promise	threaten	wish
appear	choose	expect	intend	offer	refuse	volunteer	would like
arrange	claim	fail	learn	pay	request	wait	yearn
ask	consent	grow	manage	plan	seem		
attempt	decide	hesitate	mean	prepare	struggle		

VERBS FOLLOWED BY AN OBJECT BEFORE AN INFINITIVE*

advise	cause	enable	force	need*	persuade	require	want*
allow	challenge	encourage	hire	order	promise*	teach	warn
ask*	choose*	expect*	instruct	pay*	remind	tell	wish*
beg	convince	forbid	invite	permit	request*	urge	would like*

* In the active voice, these verbs can be followed by the infinitive without an object (example: *want to speak* or *want someone to speak*).

VERBS THAT CAN BE FOLLOWED BY A GERUND OR AN INFINITIVE

with a change in meaning

forget	remember
regret	stop

without a change in meaning

begin	continue	like	prefer	try
can't stand	hate	love	start	

ADJECTIVES FOLLOWED BY AN INFINITIVE*

afraid	ashamed	depressed	eager	fortunate	lucky	relieved	surprised
alarmed	certain	determined	easy	glad	pleased	reluctant	touched
amazed	content	disappointed	embarrased	happy	prepared	sad	upset
angry	curious	distressed	encouraged	hesitant	proud	shocked	willing
anxious	delighted	disturbed	excited	likely	ready	sorry	

*Example: *I'm willing* ***to accept*** *that.*

PARTICIPIAL ADJECTIVES*

alarming –	alarmed	embarrassing –	embarrassed	paralyzing –	paralyzed
amazing –	amazed	enlightening –	enlightened	pleasing –	pleased
amusing –	amused	entertaining –	entertained	relaxing –	relaxed
annoying –	annoyed	exciting –	excited	satisfying –	satisfied
astonishing –	astonished	exhausting –	exhausted	shocking –	shocked
boring –	bored	fascinating –	fascinated	soothing –	soothed
confusing –	confused	frightening –	frightened	startling –	startled
depressing –	depressed	horrifying –	horrified	stimulating –	stimulated
disappointing –	disappointed	inspiring –	inspired	surprising –	surprised
disgusting –	disgusted	interesting –	interested	terrifying –	terrified
distressing –	distressed	irritating –	irritated	tiring –	tired
disturbing –	disturbed	moving –	moved	touching –	touched

STATIVE VERBS

amaze	contain	feel*	look like	please	smell*
appear*	cost	forget	look*	possess	sound
appreciate	desire	hate	love	prefer	suppose
astonish	dislike	have*	matter	realize	surprise
be*	doubt	hear	mean	recognize	taste*
believe	envy	imagine	mind	remember*	think*
belong	equal	include*	need	resemble	understand
care	exist	know	owe	see*	want*
consist of	fear	like	own	seem	weigh*

*These verbs also have action meanings. Example: *I see a tree.* (non-action) *I'm seeing her tomorrow.* (action)

TRANSITIVE PHRASAL VERBS

Abbreviations
s.o. = someone
sth. = something
e.g. = for example
inf. = informal

Some transitive phrasal verbs have more than one meaning. Not all are included here.

SEPARABLE

blow sth. **out** stop a flame by blowing on it
blow sth. **up** **1** make sth. explode **2** fill sth. with air, e.g., a balloon **3** make sth. larger, e.g., a photo
bring sth. **about** make sth. happen
bring sth. **back** **1** return sth. to a store **2** revive or renew sth., e.g., a custom or tradition
bring sth. **out** **1** introduce a new product **2** make a quality more noticeable
bring s.o. **up** raise a child
bring sth. **up** start to talk about an issue
burn sth. **down** burn a structure completely
call s.o. **back** return a phone call
call sth. **off** cancel sth.
call s.o. **up** call s.o. on the phone
carry sth. **out** conduct a plan
check s.o./sth. **out** look at s.o. or sth. more closely
cheer s.o. **up** make s.o. feel happier
clean s.o./sth. **up** clean s.o. or sth. completely
clear sth. **up** clarify sth.
close sth. **down** force a business or institution to close
cover sth. **up** **1** cover sth. completely **2** change facts to avoid responsibility
cross sth. **out** draw a line through sth.
cut sth. **down** make sth. fall by cutting, e.g., a tree
cut sth. **off** **1** remove sth. by cutting **2** stop the supply of sth.
cut s.o. **off** interrupt s.o who is speaking
dream sth. **up** invent or think of a new idea
drink sth. **up** drink a beverage completely
drop s.o./sth. **off** leave s.o. or sth. somewhere
empty sth. **out** empty sth. completely
figure s.o./sth. **out** understand s.o. or sth. after some thought
fill s.o. **in** tell s.o. about recent events
fill sth. **out** complete a form
fill sth. **up** fill a container completely
find sth. **out** learn new information
follow sth. **through** do everything to complete a task
get sth. **across** help s.o. understand an idea
give sth. **away** give sth. you do not need or want
give sth. **back** return sth. to its owner
give sth. **out** distribute sth.
give sth. **up** quit doing sth.
hand sth. **in** submit work, e.g., to a boss or a teacher
hand sth. **out** distribute sth.
hang sth. **up** put sth. on a hanger or hook, e.g., clothes
help s.o. **out** assist s.o.
keep s.o./sth. **away** cause s.o. or sth. to stay at a distance
lay s.o. **off** fire s.o. because of economic conditions
leave sth. **on** **1** not turn sth. off, e.g., an appliance **2** not remove sth. such as clothing or jewelry
leave sth. **out** omit sth.
let s.o. **down** disappoint s.o.
let s.o./sth. **in** allow s.o. or sth. to enter
let s.o. **off** allow s.o. to leave a bus, car, taxi, etc.
let s.o./sth. **out** allow s.o. or sth. to leave
light sth. **up** illuminate sth.
look s.o./sth. **over** examine s.o. or sth.
look s.o./sth. **up** **1** try to find s.o. **2** try to find sth. in a book, the Internet, etc.
make sth. **up** create a fictional story
pass sth. **out** distribute sth.
pass sth. **up** decide not to take an opportunity
pay s.o. **off** bribe s.o.
pay sth. **off** pay back money one owes
pick s.o./sth. **out** identify or choose s.o. or sth.
pick s.o. **up** stop a vehicle so s.o. can get in
pick s.o./sth. **up** lift s.o. or sth.
pick sth. **up** **1** get or buy sth. from somewhere **2** learn sth. new **3** get an infectious disease
point s.o./sth. **out** show s.o or sth. to another person
put sth. **away** put sth. in its appropriate place
put sth. **back** return sth. to its original place
put s.o./sth. **down** **1** stop holding or lifting s.o. or sth. **2** insult s.o.
put sth. **off** delay or postpone sth.
put sth. **on** get dressed or place sth. on one's body
put sth. **together** **1** put sth. on a wall **2** build sth.
put sth. **up** build or erect sth.
set sth. **off** cause sth. to explode
set sth. **up** **1** establish a new business, organization, etc. **2** prepare equipment for use
show s.o./sth. **off** display the best qualities of s.o. or sth.
shut sth. **off** stop a machine or supply
straighten sth. **up** make sth. neat
switch sth. **on** start a machine, turn on a light, etc.
take sth. **away** remove sth.
take sth. **back** **1** return sth. to a store **2** accept sth. returned by another person
take sth. **down** remove sth. that is hanging
take sth. **in** **1** notice and remember sth. **2** make a clothing item smaller
take sth. **off** remove clothing, jewelry, etc.
take s.o. **on** hire s.o.
take sth. **on** agree to do a task
take s.o. **out** invite s.o. somewhere and pay for his/her meal, show, etc.
take sth. **up** start doing an activity habitually
talk sth. **over** discuss sth.
tear sth. **down** destroy sth.

tear sth. **up** tear sth. into small pieces
think sth. **over** consider sth.
think sth. **up** invent or think of a new idea
throw sth. **away** put sth. in the garbage
throw sth. **out** put sth. in the garbage
touch sth. **up** improve sth. with very small changes
try sth. **on** try clothing to see if it fits
try sth. **out** use sth. to see if one likes it or if it works
turn sth. **around** **1** turn so the front is at the back **2** cause things to get better
turn s.o./sth. **down** reject s.o. or sth.
turn sth. **down** lower the volume, heat, etc.
turn sth. **in** submit a paper, application, etc.
turn sth. **off** stop a machine, light, etc.
turn s.o. **off** cause s.o. to lose interest (inf.)
turn sth. **on** start a machine, light, etc.
turn sth. **out** make or manufacture sth.
turn sth. **over** turn sth. so the bottom is at the top
turn sth. **up** raise the volume, heat, etc.
use sth. **up** use sth. completely
wake s.o. **up** cause s.o. to stop sleeping
wipe sth. **out** remove or destroy sth.
work sth. **out** **1** resolve a problem **2** calculate a math problem
write sth. **down** write sth. to have a record of it

ALWAYS SEPARATED

ask s.o. **over** invite s.o. to one's home
bring s.o./sth. **down** remove a ruler or government from power
do sth. **over** do sth. again
keep sth. **on** not remove sth. such as clothing or jewelry
see sth. **through** complete a task
start sth. **over** begin sth. again
talk s.o. **into** sth. persuade s.o. to do sth.

INSEPARABLE

cater to s.o. provide what s.o. wants or needs
carry on sth. continue sth. another person has started
come across s.o./sth. find s.o. or sth. unexpectedly
count on s.o./sth. depend on s.o. or sth.
do without s.o./sth. live without s.o. or sth. one needs or wants
go after s.o./sth. pursue s.o. or sth.
go over sth. examine sth. carefully
go without sth. live without sth. one needs or wants
run into s.o. meet s.o. unexpectedly
run into sth. accidentally hit or crash into sth.
stick with s.o. stay close to s.o.
stick with sth. continue doing sth. as before

INTRANSITIVE PHRASAL VERBS

Some intransitive phrasal verbs have more than one meaning. Not all are included here.

blow up **1** explode **2** suddenly become very angry
break down stop functioning
break out start suddenly, e.g., a war, disease, or fire
burn down burn completely
call back return a phone call
carry on **1** continue doing sth. **2** behave in a silly or emotional way
catch on become popular
check in report one's arrival at an airport or hotel
check out pay one's bill and leave a hotel
cheer up become happier
clear up become better, e.g., a rash or the weather
close down stop operating, e.g., a factory or a school
come along accompany s.o.
come back return
come in enter
come off become unattached
come out **1** appear, e.g., the sun **2** be removed, e.g., a stain
dress up wear more formal clothes or a costume
drop in visit unexpectedly
drop out quit a class, school, or program
eat out eat in a restaurant
empty out empty completely
fall off become unattached
fill out become bigger
fill up become completely full
find out learn new information
follow through continue working on sth. until it is completed
fool around have fun or not be serious
get ahead make progress or succeed
get along to not argue
get back return from a place
get together meet somewhere with a friend or acquaintance
get up get out of bed
give up quit
go along **1** accompany s.o. **2** agree
go back return
go off explode; make a sudden noise
go on continue to talk about or describe sth.
go out **1** leave a building **2** leave one's home to meet people, enjoy entertainment, etc.
go up be built
grow up become an adult
help out do sth. helpful
hang up end a phone call
hold on wait during a phone call
keep away stay at a distance
keep on continue
keep up go or think as fast as another person
lie down rest on a bed
light up **1** begin to shine brightly **2** look pleased or happy
make up end an argument and reestablish a friendly relationship
pass out become unconscious
pay off be worthwhile
pick up improve, e.g., the economy
play around have fun or not be serious
run out no longer in supply
show up appear
sign up register
sit down sit
slip up make a mistake
stand up rise to one's feet
start over begin again
stay up not go to bed
straighten up make neat
take off depart by plane
turn in go to bed (inf.)
turn out have a particular result
turn up appear
wake up stop sleeping
watch out be careful
work out **1** exercise **2** be resolved; end successfully

THREE-WORD PHRASAL VERBS

Some three-word phrasal verbs have more than one meaning. Not all are included here.

catch up on sth. **1** do sth. one didn't have time to do earlier
2 get the most recent information
catch up with s.o. exchange information about recent activities
check up on s.o. make sure s.o. is OK
come away with sth. learn sth. useful from s.o. or sth.
come down to sth. be the most important point or idea
come down with sth. get an illness
come up against s.o./sth. be faced with a difficult person or situation
come up with sth. think of an idea, plan, or solution
face up to sth. accept an unpleasant truth
fall back on sth. use an old idea because new ideas have failed
follow through on sth. continue doing sth. until it is completed
get around to sth. finally do sth.
get away with sth. avoid the consequences of a wrong act
get back at s.o. harm s.o. because he / she harmed you
give up on s.o. stop hoping that s.o. will change
give up on sth. stop trying to make sth. happen
go along with sth. agree to do sth.
go through with sth. do sth. difficult or painful
grow out of sth. stop doing sth. as one becomes an adult
keep up with s.o. stay in regular contact
look down on s.o. think one is better than another person
look out for s.o. protect s.o.
look up to s.o. admire or respect s.o.
make up for sth. do sth. to apologize
put up with s.o./sth. accept s.o. or sth. without complaining
run out of sth. no longer have enough of sth.
stand up for sth. support an idea or a principle
stand up to s.o. refuse to let s.o. treat anyone badly
team up with s.o. do a task together
think back on s.o./sth. think about and remember s.o. or sth.
walk out on s.o. end a relationship with a wife, boyfriend, etc.
watch out for s.o./sth. protect s.o. or sth.

Verb forms: overview

SUMMARY OF VERB FORMS

	Present time	Past time	Future time
Simple	**Simple present** walk / walks	**Simple past** walked	**Simple future** will walk
Continuous	**Present continuous** am walking / is walking / are walking	**Past continuous** was walking / were walking	**Future continuous** will be walking
Perfect	**Present perfect** have walked / has walked	**Past perfect** had walked	**Future perfect** will have walked
Perfect continuous	**Present perfect continuous** have been walking / has been walking	**Past perfect continuous** had been walking	**Future perfect continuous** will have been walking

SIMPLE VERB FORMS: USAGE

	Present time	Past time	Future time
Simple verb forms describe habitual actions or events that occur at a definite time.	**Simple present**[1] **Habitual action** *The department* ***meets*** *once a month to review the status of projects.* **Facts and generalizations** *The Earth* ***rotates*** *around the sun every 365 days.*	**Simple past** **Completed action that occurred at a definite time in the past** *Last year researchers* ***discovered*** *a new cancer treatment.* **Habitual action in the past**[2] *When I was young we* ***visited*** *my grandparents every week.*	**Simple future**[3] **Action that will occur at a definite time in the future** *Next year they* ***will offer*** *a course on global trade.* **Habitual action in the future** *Next month I'****ll go*** *to the gym three times a week.*

[1] The simple present tense can also express a future action: *Her flight arrives this evening at eight.*
[2] Used to and would also express habitual actions in the past: *When I was a child, we used to spend the summer in the mountains. In the mornings we would go hiking and in the afternoons we would swim in a nearby lake.*
[3] Be going to can also express a future action: *Next year they are going to offer a course on global trade.*

CONTINUOUS VERB FORMS: USAGE

	Present time	Past time	Future time
Continuous verb forms describe continuous actions or events that occur at a definite time.	**Present continuous*** **Action in progress now** *The business managers **are discussing** next year's budget right now.*	**Past continuous** **Action in progress at a definite time in the past** *None of the computers **were working** when I came in this morning.*	**Future continuous** **Action that will be in progress during a definite time in the future** *We'**ll be listening** to the speech when you arrive.*

*The present continuous can also express a future plan: *They're getting married next month.*

PERFECT VERB FORMS: USAGE

	Present time	Past time	Future time
Perfect verb forms describe actions or events in relation to other time frames.	**Present perfect*** **Completed action that occurred at an indefinite time before the present** *She **has made** many contributions to the field.* **Recently completed action** *He **has** just **published** an article about his findings.* **Uncompleted action (action that began in the past, continues into the present, and may continue into the future)** *They **have studied** ancient cultures for many years.*	**Past perfect** **Action that occurred at some point before a definite time in the past** *By 2016, he **had started** a new business.* **Action that occurred before another past action** *They **had** already **finished** medical school when the war broke out.*	**Future perfect** **Action that will be completed by some point at a definite time in the future** *By this time next year, I **will have completed** my research.*

*Many statements in the present perfect can also be stated correctly using the simple past tense, depending on the speaker's perspective: *She made many contributions to the field.*

PERFECT CONTINUOUS VERB FORMS: USAGE

	Present time	Past time	Future time
Perfect continuous verb forms describe continuous actions or events in relation to other time frames.	**Present perfect continuous** **Uncompleted continuous action (action that began in the past, continues into the present, and may continue into the future)** *She **has been lecturing** about that topic since 2015.* **Very recently completed action** *The workers **have been protesting**. They're finished now.*	**Past perfect continuous** **Continuous action that occurred before another past action or time** *By 2015, researchers **had been seeking** a cure for AIDS for more than thirty years.*	**Future perfect continuous** **Continuous action that occurred before another action or time in the future** *When the new director takes over, I **will have been working** at this company for ten years.*

Grammar Booster

The Grammar Booster is optional. It provides more explanation and practice, as well as additional related grammar concepts and review.

UNIT 1

Describing past actions and events: review

The past of be and the simple past tense

Use for completed actions and states that occurred at a specific time in the past.

He **was** here at 10:00 and **left** this message.

The past continuous

Use for one or more recurring actions or actions in progress at a specific time in the past.

Steven **was** always **talking** in class.

The baby **was sleeping** and the older children **were eating** dinner when we arrived.

The present perfect

Use for actions completed at an unspecified time in the past.

She **has** already **informed** her manager about the problem.

New York **has been called** the capital of the world.

The past perfect

Use for an action that occurred before another past action.

They **had** already **made** a decision when we called.

The past perfect continuous

Use for a continuing action that was occurring before another past action.

We **had been working** for two hours when the storm began.

Used to / would

Use used to for past situations and habits that no longer exist. Use would or used to for actions that were repeated regularly in the past.

When she was younger, she never **used to be** afraid of anything.

In those days, we **would** (or **used to**) **take** a long walk every evening.

The future as seen from the past

Use was / were going to + the base form of a verb to express future plans someone had in the past.

He **was going to start** his own business, but he couldn't get a loan.

Would + the base form of the verb can also express the future as seen from the past, but only after statements of knowledge or belief.

We always thought that she **would become** an actor, but she decided to study law.

A Correct the errors with past forms.

1 Florence has been walking for several hours before she realized that her wallet was missing.

2 As a child, he was practicing the piano for hours every day. Then he stopped taking lessons.

3 "I have seen that movie last year, and I thought it was great," Frank exclaimed.

4 Before this morning, I never took a yoga class.

5 He was working on the problem all morning when he finally found the solution.

6 My husband believed he will never get married, but then he met me.

Stative verbs

Stative (non-action) verbs express mental states, emotions, perceptions, descriptions, relationships, possession, measurements, and other conditions, rather than actions. They are not usually used in continuous verb forms, even when they describe a situation in progress.

Many people **believe** the environment should be our top priority. NOT Many people ~~are believing~~ the environment should be our top priority.

She **has** always **understood** that job satisfaction was important. NOT She ~~has always been understanding~~ that job satisfaction was important.

Some stative verbs have both non-action and action meanings. A stative verb that has an action meaning may be used in the continuous.

Non-action meaning	Action meaning
That**'s** ridiculous! (description)	You**'re being** ridiculous! (act in a ridiculous way)
She **has** two children. (possession)	She**'s having** another baby soon. (act of giving birth)
We **think** these laws are unfair. (mental state: opinion)	We**'re thinking** of organizing a protest. (act of planning)
How does the soup **taste**? (perception)	I**'m tasting** the soup to see if it needs salt. (act of tasting)
This garden **looks** neglected. (description)	The child **is looking** at the flowers. (act of looking)

NOTE: In informal spoken English, certain stative verbs, especially want, need, and have to, are becoming common in the continuous:

I**'m** really **wanting** a cup of good coffee. Let's go into that coffee bar.

For a complete list of stative verbs, see the Reference Charts, page 124.

B **Decide if each stative verb in parentheses has an action or a non-action meaning. Then complete each sentence with the simple present tense or the present continuous.**

	action	non-action	
1	☐	☐	Sara .... (doubt) that she'll get a promotion at her job.
2	☐	☐	Our skills are excellent, and we .... (have) experience in the field.
3	☐	☐	Philip .... (think) about moving abroad to teach for a year.
4	☐	☐	We .... (have) dinner at 6:00 today so we can go to the lecture on climate change.
5	☐	☐	Michael .... (not remember) where the meeting will take place.
6	☐	☐	The book .... (include) some diagrams to support the hypothesis.
7	☐	☐	The doctor .... (see) another patient now.

UNIT 2

Adjective clauses: overview

Purpose	Examples
To identify or give additional information about a person · relative pronoun can be subject or object of clause	The physicist {**who** / **that**} **made that discovery** teaches at my university. The psychologist {**whom** / **that** / **who**} **he interviewed** did a study about lying.
To identify or give additional information about a place or thing · relative pronoun can be subject or object of clause	The building {**that** / **which**} **is on your left** was formerly a bank. The article {**(that)*** / **(which)***} **I read yesterday** is fascinating.
To show possession	The woman **whose house you admired** is a famous author. Paris, **whose museums hold so many treasures**, is a favorite destination for tourists.
To modify a noun of place	The town {**where they live** / **in which they live** / **that they live in** / **which they live in**} has many beautiful parks and squares.
To modify a noun of time	I can't remember the year {**(when)*** / **(that)*** / **(in which)***} **we visited them for the first time.**

*Note: These relative pronouns may be omitted.

A **Underline the best word or words to complete each sentence.**

1 Parents (who / which) spend time with their children give them a sense of security.
2 The city (that / in which) my father grew up was destroyed during the war.
3 The Miller family, (whose / who) house is for sale, hopes to find a buyer soon.
4 The star of the film, (whom / which) we had hoped to meet, didn't come to the reception.
5 I will never forget the time (when / who) I told the truth and was punished for it.
6 The woman (who / which) used to teach English at my school is now the director there.
7 The *Sun Times*, (whose / which) is the best newspaper in town, recently published an article about the social uses of lying.

Grammar for Writing: adjective clauses with quantifiers

Some adjective clauses may include a quantifier that refers to a previously mentioned noun or noun phrase. These clauses are constructed as follows: quantifier + of + relative pronoun (whom, which, or whose).

He consulted three doctors, **all of whom** confirmed the original diagnosis.

I can think of several possible explanations, **none of which** justifies their behavior.

The reporters questioned the president, **one of whose** strengths is his ability to remain calm under pressure.

Adjective clauses that include quantifiers appear more often in written than spoken English.

Some expressions of quantity used with of

a few of	half of	none of
all of	little of	one of
a number of	many of	several of
both of	most of	some of
each of	neither of	

B Complete each sentence with a quantifier from the box and the correct relative pronoun. Use each quantifier only once.

all of	each of	neither of	one of	both of

1 I've bought several of the company's products, only .... works.

2 He's upset with all three of his children, ... makes up a different excuse to avoid sharing chores at home.

3 The teacher sent six of her students to speak with the director, ... were caught cheating on the test.

4 The two articles, ... deal with the issue of honesty in the workplace, should be required reading for everyone in the company.

5 My parents, ... has ever told a lie, are the most honest people I know.

Grammar for Writing: reduced adjective clauses

Adjective clauses can be reduced to adjective phrases.

clause: Hawaii, **which is known for its beautiful topography and climate**, lies in the middle of the Pacific Ocean.

phrase: Hawaii, **known for its beautiful topography and climate**, lies in the middle of the Pacific Ocean.

There are two ways to reduce an adjective clause to an adjective phrase:

1 **When the adjective clause contains a form of the verb be, drop the relative pronoun and the verb be.**

Herodotus, **who was the first Greek historian**, wrote about the wars between ancient Greece and Persia. →

Herodotus, **the first Greek historian**, wrote about the wars between ancient Greece and Persia.

2 **When the adjective clause does not contain a form of the verb be, drop the relative pronoun and use the present participle of the verb.**

The human skeleton, **which contains** 206 separate bones, is a strong and flexible structure. →

The human skeleton, **containing** 206 separate bones, is a strong and flexible structure.

Those **who tamper** with the smoke detector will be prosecuted. →

Those **tampering** with the smoke detector will be prosecuted.

Remember

A clause is a group of words that has both a subject and a verb.

A phrase is a group of words that doesn't have both a subject and a verb.

Adjective phrases often begin with an article or one, a type of, or a kind of.

My grandmother, **a very practical and hardworking woman**, made clothes for the entire family.

The largest city in Turkey, Istanbul is at the point where Europe joins Asia.

They're looking for a quiet place to live, preferably **one in the suburbs**.

Chanterelles, **a type of edible mushroom with a rich yellow color**, are very expensive.

The llama and alpaca are camelids, **a kind of mammal native to South America**.

The use of commas in reduced adjective clauses follows the same rules as those for full adjective clauses. See page 000 for the use of commas in restrictive and non-restrictive adjective clauses.

C Reduce the adjective clause in each sentence to an adjective phrase.

1 Daniel Craig and Rachel Weisz, who are two of the U.K.'s best-known movie actors, do charity work with underprivileged teens.

2 Philanthropy, which is the act of giving time and money to help others, can be very time-consuming.

3 Executives who fail to accept responsibility for their mistakes risk losing the trust of their employees.

4 The United Nations, which hosts a number of humanitarian organizations, invited Angelina Jolie to be a goodwill ambassador to countries in need of assistance.

5 Truthfulness, which is believed to be taught to us by our parents, develops in children from a very young age.

D **On a separate sheet of paper, combine each pair of sentences. Use the second sentence as an adjective phrase.**

1 Amal Hijazi is also known for her humanitarian work. (Hijazi is a Lebanese pop singer currently living in Beirut.)

Amal Hijazi, a Lebanese pop singer currently living in Beirut, is also known for her humanitarian work.

2 Telling a white lie can still get us into big trouble. (A white lie is the type of lie we tell to protect others.)

3 My mother taught me a lot about how to be honest. (My mother is the only person I know who is unable to tell a lie.)

4 My brother frequently volunteers in a hospital. (My brother is a man of great compassion.)

5 A lot of money was raised at last night's concert. (Last night's concert was the biggest charity event of the year.)

UNIT 3

Embedded questions: review and common errors

Remember: A question can be embedded in a noun clause.
Use if or whether to begin an embedded yes / no question.
If and whether have the same meaning.

Yes / no questions	Embedded yes / no questions
Does she get fed up when she's frustrated?	Let's ask **whether she gets fed up when she's frustrated**.
Do you know what I mean?	I'd like to know **if you know what I mean**.
Have you ever asked your boss for a raise?	Could you tell me **if you've ever asked your boss for a raise?**

Use a question word to begin embedded information questions.

Information questions	Embedded information questions
What's she afraid of?	I can't remember **what she's afraid of**.
Why have you decided to stay home?	I don't understand **why you've decided to stay home**.
When was it found?	Do you know **when it was found**?

Phrases that are often followed by embedded questions

Ask ...	I'd like to know ...
Tell me ...	Don't tell them ...
I wonder ...	I can't remember ...
Let's ask ...	Do you know ...?
Don't say ...	Can you tell me ...?
I don't know ...	Can you remember ...?
Let me know ...	Could you explain ...?

Question words and phrases

how	what color	which
how many	what day	who
how much	when	whom
what	where	why

Punctuation of embedded questions

Use a period with an embedded question within a statement.
Use a question mark with an embedded question within a question.

I don't know who is singing. **Would you mind telling me** who is singing?

Social use of embedded questions

You can use an embedded question to soften a direct question.

Why isn't this printer working? → Can you tell me **why this printer isn't working**?
Where's the bathroom? → Do you know **where the bathroom is**?

Embedded questions: common errors

Remember: Use regular statement word order, not inverted (question) word order, in embedded questions.

Do you know **why your parents won't** fly? NOT Do you know why ~~won't they~~ fly?
Can you tell me **whether this bus runs** express? NOT Can you tell me ~~does this bus run~~ express?

A **On a separate sheet of paper, combine the two parts of each item to write an embedded question, using if or whether, as indicated. Punctuate each sentence correctly.**

1 I can't remember (Is there going to be a late show?) [whether]

2 We're not sure (Was it John or Bill who found the wallet?) [whether]

3 Could you tell me (Is the movie going to start soon?) [if]

4 I wonder (Will the traffic be bad at this hour?) [if]

5 Would she like to know (Is there a possibility of getting a seat on the plane?) [if]

6 Do you know (Does this movie have a good cast?) [whether]

B **On a separate sheet of paper, combine the two parts of each item to write an embedded question. Punctuate each sentence correctly.**

1 Please let me know (When do you expect to arrive?)
2 I wonder (Where were your parents when the earthquake occurred?)
3 Can you tell me (How do you know that?)
4 We're not sure (Where can we buy flowers to take to the hostess of the dinner party?)
5 They'd like to understand (Why don't you just call the restaurant for reservations?)
6 Please tell us (What time does the performance begin?)

C **On a separate sheet of paper, rewrite the sentences, correcting errors, including punctuation errors.**

1 Please tell me what do you usually say when you feel frustrated.
2 Can you remind me what day is the party?
3 Could you explain how did you make this omelet?
4 Tell me what is your favorite color?
5 I wonder what should they do.
6 Do you think is something wrong?

Count and non-count nouns

Non-count nouns made countable

A non-count noun is neither singular nor plural. Except in certain circumstances, it is not preceded by an article.
A non-count noun can be preceded by certain quantifiers such as much, a lot of, a little, and some.

I always like **a little** sugar in my oatmeal. NOT I like ~~a sugar~~ in my oatmeal. OR Sugar ~~are~~ good in oatmeal.

Many non-count nouns can be made countable by using a phrase to limit them or give them a form.

If you want to serve fruit for dessert, serve each person **two pieces of** fruit instead of one. One piece might not be enough.
They got scared when they heard **a clap of** thunder.

Some phrases to make non-count nouns countable

The following phrases are used to make non-count nouns countable. The list includes abstract ideas, natural phenomena, foods, drinks and liquids, and household products. Many phrases are used in more than one category.

- **an article of** (clothing)
- **a bar of** (chocolate / soap)
- **a bottle of** (water)
- **a bowl of** (rice / soup / cereal)
- **a box of** (rice / pasta)
- **a carton of** (milk / juice)
- **a cloud of** (smoke)
- **a cup of** (sugar / rice / coffee / tea)
- **a drop of** (rain / water)
- **a game of** (tennis / soccer / chess)
- **a glass of** (juice / milk)
- **a grain of** (sand / salt / rice)
- **a liter of** (gasoline / oil)
- **a loaf of** (bread)
- **a piece of** (fruit / paper / wood / metal / advice)
- **a teaspoon of** (salt / sugar)
- **a type (or kind) of** (energy / behavior / music)

Phrases that are used to make a number of non-count nouns countable

Here are four common phrases that are used to make a number of non-count nouns countable.

a piece of	**a sense of**	**an act of**	**a state of**
advice	achievement	anger	confusion
equipment	community	defiance	disrepair
furniture	confidence	generosity	emergency
gossip	control	insanity	mind
information	humor	justice	war
news	heroism	kindness	
paper	identity		

Nouns used in both countable and uncountable sense

Some nouns can be used in both a countable and an uncountable sense.

a chance	=	a possibility	a coffee	=	a cup of coffee
chance	=	luck	coffee	=	a type of beverage
a light	=	a light source, such as a light bulb, lamp, etc.	a hair	=	a single hair
light	=	a type of energy	hair	=	all the hair on the head
a metal	=	a specific substance, such as gold or steel	a shampoo	=	a brand of shampoo
metal	=	a type of substance	shampoo	=	soap for your hair

D **On a separate sheet of paper, rewrite the statements, using a phrase to make each underlined non-count noun countable.**

1 If you're going to play tennis tomorrow morning, give me a call.
2 When I plant my garden in April, I wait eagerly for the first rain to make sure the plants grow.
3 If you sew or repair clothing yourself instead of taking it to someone else, you will save a lot of money in the long run.
4 They say that turning bread upside down after a slice has been cut from it will keep it fresh.
5 When I make chicken soup, I like to serve rice on the side.

E **Choose the best word from the box to complete each sentence.**

act	bar	glass	piece	sense	state

1 The group's donation was a true .... of generosity.
2 My sister has an amazing .... of humor.
3 The woman slipped on a .... of soap in the shower.
4 Our town has been in a .... of emergency since the hurricane.
5 The park just installed a new .... of equipment in the playground.
6 I asked the waitress for a .... of orange juice.

UNIT 4

Grammar for Writing: more conjunctions and transitions

Purpose	Coordinating conjunctions	Subordinating conjunctions	Transitions
To add information *Marc is working as a photographer,* ***and*** *he has experience in graphic design.* ***In addition to*** *working as a photographer, Marc has experience in graphic design.*	and	in addition to besides	In addition, Furthermore, Moreover, Besides, More importantly,
To clarify information *Smaller cars are more efficient;* ***in other words,*** *they use less fuel.*			That is, In other words, In fact,
To illustrate or exemplify information *Many European cities are found along waterways.* ***For example,*** *London, Paris, Vienna, and Budapest all lie on major rivers.*			For instance, For example, To illustrate,
To show contrast *Meg does not usually perform well under pressure,* ***but*** *she gave a brilliant recital.* *Meg does not usually perform well under pressure.* ***Despite this,*** *she gave a brilliant recital.*	but yet	even though although though while whereas despite the fact that	However, Nevertheless, Nonetheless, In contrast, Even so, Still, Despite [this / that], In spite of [this / that], All the same, On the other hand,
To express cause or result *They have a new baby,* ***so*** *they rarely get a good night's sleep!* ***Now that*** *they have a new baby, they rarely get a good night's sleep!*	so for	because since due to the fact that now that so that	Therefore, Consequently, Accordingly, As a consequence, As a result,

Remember

- A coordinating conjunction links two independent clauses in a sentence. It is preceded by a comma.
- A subordinating conjunction introduces a dependent clause in a sentence. When a dependent clause starts a sentence, the clause is followed by a comma.
- A transition links ideas between sentences or paragraphs. It usually begins a sentence and is followed by a comma. A transition can be preceded by a semicolon.

To express a condition *Pollution can be reduced* ***provided that*** *car manufacturers mass-produce cars with greater fuel efficiency.* *Car manufacturers should mass-produce cars with greater fuel efficiency.* ***Otherwise,*** *pollution will not be reduced.*	or (else)	(only) if provided that as long as unless even if whether (or not)	Otherwise,
To show similarity *Water is necessary for life.* ***Similarly,*** *oxygen is required by all living things.*			Similarly, Likewise,

A **On a separate sheet of paper, combine each pair of sentences two ways: once with the connecting word(s) in a and once with the connecting words in b. Use a semicolon before a transition. Change the wording as necessary to retain the meaning.**

1 John is a bit of a perfectionist. His brothers are pretty easygoing. (**a** while **b** in contrast)

2 Nicole has always struggled with being disorganized. She has made a lot of progress recently. (**a** although **b** despite that)

3 My boss tends to be very negative. He gets angry too quickly. (**a** in addition to **b** furthermore)

4 I need to stop procrastinating. I won't ever finish the class assignment on time. (**a** unless **b** otherwise)

5 Carla has been trying not to be so controlling at work. She gets along better with her colleagues. (**a** now that **b** as a result)

Cleft sentences: more on meaning and use

Cleft sentences with What

Cleft sentences with What are often used to clarify what someone said, thought, or meant.

A: Do you think Gail would like to go somewhere for her birthday?
B: Actually, **what she'd really like is** for us to take her out to a nice restaurant.

A: Were you surprised that Rob called you after your argument?
B: Actually, **what surprised me was** that he was even willing to talk to me!

Cleft sentences with It

Cleft sentences with It are used to clarify who, what, when, where, or why.

A: Did you try calling me a few minutes ago? Your number popped up in my missed calls.
B: Actually, **it was my sister** who called you. She was using my phone. (clarifies who)

A: Our neighbor had a great party last night. But I have to say, the noise really got to me.
B: Well, **it was not getting an invitation** that really bugged me. (clarifies what)

A: Don't I see you in the computer lab on Mondays?
B: I doubt it. **It's usually on Tuesdays and Thursdays** that I go to the lab. (clarifies when)

A: Did you hear about the bus accident this morning?
B: Yeah. And **it was just down the street from me** where it happened! (clarifies where)

A: Thanks for helping me with the homework.
B: Well, **it's because you're always so nice** that I did it. (clarifies why)

B **Clarify what B said, thought, or meant. Complete each cleft sentence using the underlined information.**

1 **A:** Are you excited about going on vacation next week?
B: Actually, ... getting to see my aunt and uncle again.

2 **A:** Did you think your boss was going to lose her temper?
B: On the contrary. .... that she was going to give me a promotion.

3 **A:** It's 6:15. I thought you said you'd be here at 6:00.
B: .... we should plan to meet at 6:00, but that I might be a little late.

4 **A:** What did Gary mean when he said his tablet cost an arm and a leg?

B: .... it was a lot more expensive than he thought it would be.

5 **A:** Should you be eating that cake?

B: According to my doctor, ... nothing but healthy food. But I don't care!

C **Write cleft sentences with It to clarify who, what, when, where, or why. Use the prompts.**

1 **A:** Is feeding a parrot a lot of work?

B: Are you kidding? .... (clean the cage)

2 **A:** Did Gina write that song?

B: No. .... (her sister)

3 **A:** Will the traffic be really bad at this time?

B: I don't think so. .... (at 5:00)

4 **A:** These cookies are so good!

B: Thanks. .... (because / I add / nuts)

5 **A:** Aren't we supposed to meet Jason at the coffee shop?

B: No. .... (at the bus stop)

UNIT 5

Indirect speech: review and expansion

Imperatives in indirect speech

When imperatives are used to report commands, requests, instructions, and invitations, the imperative form changes to the infinitive. The negative infinitive is used for negative commands, requests, and instructions.

Direct speech	Indirect speech
"Could you please **go** to the store?"	She asked me **to go** to the store.
The chef said, "**Add** two eggs and stir the mixture."	The chef said **to add** two eggs and stir the mixture.
"Please **have** dinner with us," he said.	He invited me **to have** dinner with them.
She told the child, "**Don't cross** the street."	She told the child **not to cross** the street.

Remember
Indirect questions end with a period, not a question mark. Like in embedded questions, verbs in indirect questions follow the same changes as the verbs in indirect statements.

Changes to pronouns and possessives

Remember: In indirect speech, pronouns and possessives change to reflect the point of view of the reporter rather than the original speaker.

My manager said, "**You** have to finish **your** report and give it to **me** as soon as possible."	→	My manager said (that) **I** had to finish **my** report and give it to **her** as soon as possible.
I told her, "**You**'ll have **this** report on **your** desk by noon."	→	I told her (that) **she** would have **that** report on **her** desk by noon.
Peter asked them, "Are **these** coats **yours**?"	→	Peter asked them if **those** coats were **theirs**.

A **On a separate sheet of paper, write each sentence in indirect speech.**

1 Marian advised Claire, "Turn on the TV at 9:00 because there's a funny movie on."
2 Dr. Baker advised his patient, "Don't let emotional tension make you sick."
3 She told me, "Be a good sport and laugh about it."
4 "Don't laugh at that joke," Fred instructed his son. "It's disgusting."
5 "Laugh first, cry later," an old saying advises us.
6 Lucas told us, "Never touch the green button on the printer."
7 "Take the penguin to the zoo tomorrow," Mr. Franklin's neighbor told him.
8 Nick said, "Please don't ask how the meeting went."

B On a separate sheet of paper, write these conversations in indirect speech, using correct pronouns and possessives.

1 **MARIA:** Your cartoon is great. Your drawing is so funny.
JACK: Yours is hilarious, too! It really cracked me up!

2 **KATHERINE**: Allison, I'm not sure if this tablet is yours.
ALLISON: It's definitely mine. Thanks!

3 **RICHARD:** My paper on the health benefits of humor has just been published in a medical journal.
ME: I'm happy for you! I'd appreciate it if you could give me a copy.

4 **KIM:** I bought a new MP3 player last week.
BEN: I know. I saw it on your desk. It looks much better than your old one.

5 **SAM:** I got all these articles about humor on the Internet last weekend.
PIRI: That's great. Would you let me read them when you've finished them?

Maria said Jack's cartoon was great and that ...
Jack answered that ...

Say, tell, and ask

Remember: Use tell when you mention the listener. You can use say in indirect speech when you mention the listener, but you must use the preposition to and introduce the indirect speech with that.

Marie **told** Dr. Barton she had to change the time of her appointment. (listener mentioned)
Dr. Barton **said** that wouldn't be a problem. (listener not mentioned)
Dr. Barton **said to** the nurse that it wouldn't be a problem. (listener mentioned)

Use ask either with or without mentioning the listener. Don't use to after ask when you mention the listener.

Marie **asked** if she could make an appointment later in the week. OR Marie **asked** Dr. Barton if she could make an appointment later in the week.

BE CAREFUL!
DON'T SAY: He ~~said the manager~~ that he completely disagreed with her.
DON'T SAY: He ~~told~~ that he completely disagreed with the manager.
DON'T SAY: He ~~told to the manager~~ that he completely disagreed with her.
DON'T SAY: He ~~asked to the manager~~ if she agreed.

C Complete the sentences with a form of say, tell, or ask.

1 She .... the waiter if she could pay with a credit card.
2 We .... that we would come back later when they were less busy.
3 He .... his friends that he would be a few minutes late.
4 She .... to her teacher that she needed a bit more time.
5 They .... the reporter that they were ready to provide information about the case.
6 I .... them if they enjoyed the movie.

Grammar for Writing: other reporting verbs

Writers use a variety of reporting verbs to describe actions more specifically and accurately.

claim
"Things are definitely getting better," **claims** Charles Wilder, a patient trying out humor therapy for the first time.
Charles Wilder, a patient trying out humor therapy for the first time, **claims** that things are definitely getting better.

declare
"The nursing staff has been doing a brilliant job!" **declared** the head doctor on Tuesday.
On Tuesday, the head doctor **declared** that the nursing staff had been doing a brilliant job.

explain
"You should always discuss dieting with your doctor," Dr. Fish **explained**.
Dr. Fish **explained** that people should always discuss dieting with their doctors.

report
The New York Times **reports**, "Obesity is a growing problem in Asia."
Last year, the New York Times **reported** that obesity was a growing problem in Asia.

state
The new CEO **stated**, "Things are going to change around here."
The new CEO **stated** that things were going to change at the company.

More reporting verbs

add	maintain
announce	mention
answer	promise
comment	remark
complain	reply
exclaim	reveal
imply	write

D **On a separate sheet of paper, restate each sentence with a different reporting verb. Use a dictionary if necessary.**

1 The Bangkok Post says that the president of Chile will be visiting Thailand next month.

2 The minister of education said yesterday that major improvements had been made in schools across the country.

3 The secretary of the United Nations says that more should be done to alleviate world hunger.

4 The scientists who conducted the study said that more research would have to be conducted.

5 The children who wrote on the walls said that they wouldn't do it again.

6 The BBC said that it would increase its coverage of the news in the Middle East.

Pronunciation table

These are the pronunciation symbols used in ***Summit 2***.

Vowels

Symbol	Key Word	Symbol	Key Word
i	beat, feed	ə	banana, among
ɪ	bit, did	ɚ	shirt, murder
eɪ	date, paid	aɪ	bite, cry, buy, eye
ɛ	bet, bed	aʊ	about, how
æ	bat, bad	ɔɪ	voice, boy
ɑ	box, odd, father	ɪr	beer
ɔ	bought, dog	ɛr	bare
oʊ	boat, road	ɑr	bar
ʊ	book, good	ɔr	door
u	boot, food, student	ʊr	tour
ʌ	but, mud, mother		

Consonants

Symbol	Key Word	Symbol	Key Word
p	pack, happy	z	zip, please, goes
b	back, rubber	ʃ	ship, machine, station, special, discussion
t	tie	ʒ	measure, vision
d	die	h	hot, who
k	came, key, quick	m	men, some
g	game, guest	n	sun, know, pneumonia
tʃ	church, nature, watch	ŋ	sung, ringing
dʒ	judge, general, major	w	wet, white
f	fan, photograph	l	light, long
v	van	r	right, wrong
θ	thing, breath	y	yes, use, music
ð	then, breathe	t̬	butter, bottle
s	sip, city, psychology	t̚	button

Pronunciation Booster

The Pronunciation Booster is optional. It provides a pronunciation lesson and practice to support speaking in each unit, making students' speech more comprehensible.

UNIT 1

Sentence stress and intonation: review

Sentence stress

Remember: Content words are generally stressed in a sentence.

I've **ALWAYS DREAMED** about **BEING** a **PHOTOGRAPHER**.
You've been **TALKING** about **DOING** that for **YEARS**!
Have you **EVER THOUGHT** about a **CAREER** in **LAW**?

Content words

nouns	photographer, Robert, career
verbs	think, study, discuss
adjectives	important, young, successful
adverbs	carefully, ever, recently
possessive pronouns	ours, yours, theirs
demonstrative pronouns	this, that, these
reflexive pronouns	myself, yourself, ourselves
interrogative pronouns	who, what, why

In compound nouns, stress only the first word.

She has just been accepted to a top **BUSINESS school**.
Have you made any progress with your **JOB search**?

Intonation

Lower pitch after the stressed syllable in the last stressed word in statements, commands, and information questions. Raise pitch after the last stressed syllable in yes/no questions.

I love the outdoors, so I've decided to become a naturalist.
What's stopping you?
Tell me something about your experience.
Have you made plans to get married?

If the last syllable in the sentence is stressed, lengthen the vowel and lower pitch. In yes/no questions, lengthen the vowel and raise pitch.

I just gave notice at the bank.
Have you decided on a career?

A ▶6:02 **Listen and practice.**

1 I've always dreamed about being a photographer.
2 You've been talking about doing that for years!
3 Have you ever thought about a career in law?

B ▶6:03 **Listen and practice.**

1 I love the outdoors, so I've decided to become a naturalist.
2 Tell me something about your experience.
3 What's stopping you?
4 Have you made plans to get married?
5 I just gave notice at the bank.
6 Have you decided on a career?

C **Circle the content words.**

1 It was very difficult for Dan to hide his disappointment.
2 He was rejected by two law schools.
3 What does he plan to do now?
4 He just accepted a position teaching math at the university.
5 MediLabs has an opening for a junior lab specialist.

▶6:04 **Now practice reading each sentence aloud. Listen to compare.***

D **Circle the last stressed content word in each sentence.**

1 He wants to start his own travel agency.
2 I don't really know how to get started.
3 Do I need to have experience in the tourism industry?
4 Why are you looking for a change?
5 Tell me about your plans for the coming year.
6 Do you want to become a flight attendant?
7 Have you applied for that job?

▶6:05 **Now practice reading each sentence aloud, using the intonation patterns you have learned. Listen to compare.***

UNIT 2

Emphatic stress and pitch to express emotion

Use emphatic stress and higher pitch on content words to indicate intensity of emotion.

I'm **SO SORRY**!
I'm **REALLY UPSET**!
What do you **MEAN**?
How could you **DO** that?
What **GREAT NEWS**!
Thank you **SO MUCH**!

A ▶6:06 **Listen and practice.**

1 I'm so sorry!
2 I'm really upset!
3 What do you mean?
4 How could you do that?
5 What great news!
6 Thank you so much!

B ▶6:07 **Practice reading each sentence aloud, using intonation to express emotion. Listen to compare.***

1 **JOHN**, what **HAPPENED**?
2 You look **WORRIED**.
3 I feel **JUST TERRIBLE**!
4 How did **THAT** happen?
5 Why didn't you slow **DOWN**?
6 We could have been **KILLED**!
7 How could you **SAY** that?

*NOTE: Whenever you see a listening activity with an asterisk (*), say each word, phrase, or sentence in the pause *after* the number. Then listen for confirmation.

UNIT 3

Vowel reduction to /ə/

Remember: The /u/ sound in the function word <u>to</u> is often reduced to /ə/ in spoken English.

We tried **to** cheer him up. /tə/
They were scared **to** death. /tə/
It was starting **to** get me down. /tə/
You just need **to** give it a little more time. /tə/

Function words

prepositions	of, from, at, to
conjunctions	and, but, or
determiners	a, the, some
personal pronouns	he, she, they
possessive adjectives	my, her, their
auxiliary verbs	have [+ past participle] be [+ present participle]

Do not reduce the /u/ sound when <u>to</u> comes before another /ə/ sound.

/tə/ /tu/
She was trying **to e-mail** a message **to a** friend.

Be careful! When an auxiliary verb is negative or used in short answers, it is generally stressed.

I **CAN'T GO**. He **WON'T LIKE** it.
No, they **DON'T**. Yes, I **HAVE**.

When <u>to</u> occurs before <u>her</u> or <u>him</u>, you can say it two ways (Note the change in syllable stress, too):

Use /tə/ and pronounce /h/ → I sent it **to her** yesterday. /tə'hər/
Use /tu/ and drop /h/ → I sent it **to her** yesterday. /'tuər/

In the phrases <u>have to</u>, <u>ought to</u>, and <u>be going to</u>, /u/ generally reduces to /ə/, and there are often other sound changes.

I didn't **have to** walk very far. /hæftə/
You really **ought to** be careful next time. /ɔt̬ə/
We're definitely **going to** take a cell phone on our next trip. /gʌnə/

A ▶6:08 **Listen and practice.**

1 We tried to cheer him up.
2 They were scared to death.
3 It was starting to get me down.
4 You just need to give it a little more time.
5 She was trying to e-mail a message to a friend.
6 I sent it to her yesterday.
7 I sent it to her yesterday.
8 I didn't have to walk very far.
9 You really ought to be careful next time.
10 We're definitely going to take a cell phone on our next trip.

B **Circle the words in the following sentences that you think contain sounds that will be reduced, according to what you have learned about vowel reduction.**

1 I'm learning to sail my ship.
2 They had sent an SOS text message from a cell phone to a friend in London.
3 They got several messages telling them to be strong.
4 The helicopters had been unable to take off because of the severe weather.
5 You ought to tell your brother that you can't talk to him right now.
6 Don't let it get to you.
7 I'm going to refuse to give up.
8 We have to keep trying, no matter how tired we are.

▶6:09 **Now practice reading each sentence aloud and listen to compare.***

UNIT 4

Shifting emphatic stress

You can shift stress within a sentence to change emphasis. Place emphatic stress on key words to get your meaning across.

A: I think I'm too critical of other people.
B: Really? I don't think I'm critical **ENOUGH**.

A: I don't think I'm critical enough.
B: Really? I think I'm **TOO** critical.

A: I think I'm too critical of other people.
B: I don't see you that way at all. **I'M** too critical.

A: I think I'm too critical of other people.
B: Really? Not me ... At least I don't **THINK** I'm too critical.

A ▶ 6:10 **Listen and practice.**

1 I don't think I'm critical **ENOUGH**.

2 I think I'm **TOO** critical.

3 **I'M** too critical.

4 I don't **THINK** I'm too critical.

B **Study each conversation, paying attention to emphatic stress.**

1 "You know what my problem is? I'm a perfectionist."
RESPONSE: Well, **I'M** just the opposite.

2 "You know what my problem is? I'm a perfectionist."
RESPONSE: Not me. I'm just the **OPPOSITE**.

3 "What set Sam off this morning?"
RESPONSE: I have no idea. But he's **ALWAYS** angry about **SOMETHING**.

4 "Why did Sam tell Paul off in front of everyone?"
RESPONSE: It's just the way he is. He's always **ANGRY** about something.

5 "Why was Judy so angry this morning?"
RESPONSE: I don't know. I've **NEVER** seen her lose her cool like that.

6 "Can you believe how angry Judy was this morning?"
RESPONSE: Not really. I've never seen her lose her cool like **THAT**.

▶ 6:11 **Now practice reading each response aloud, using emphatic stress as shown. Listen to compare.***

UNIT 5

Intonation of sarcasm

Saying the opposite of what you mean in order to show that you don't think a joke is funny is a type of sarcasm. When someone thinks a joke is funny, the response is usually said with raised pitch. The same response can convey sarcasm if it is said with flattened pitch and at a slower pace.

Pleasure	Sarcasm
How funny! (= It's funny.)	How funny. (= It's not funny.)
That's hysterical! (= It's funny.)	That's hysterical. (= It's not funny.)
That's terrific! (= It's great.)	That's terrific. (= It's not great.)
I love it! (= It's great.)	I love it. (= It's not great.)

A ▶ 6:12 **Listen and practice.**

1 How funny! / How funny.

2 That's hysterical! / That's hysterical.

3 That's terrific! / That's terrific.

4 I love it! / I love it.

B ▶ 6:13 **Practice saying each statement two ways, first with intonation showing pleasure and then sarcasm. Listen to compare.* (Note that your choices may differ from what you hear on the audio.)**

1 That's hilarious! / That's hilarious.

2 That's so funny! / That's so funny.

3 What a funny story! / What a funny story.

4 That's great! / That's great.

5 That's too much! / That's too much.

6 That really made me laugh! / That really made me laugh.

Test-Taking Skills Booster

The Test-Taking Skills Booster is optional. It provides practice in applying some key logical thinking and comprehension skills typically included in reading and listening tasks on standardized proficiency tests. Each unit contains one Reading Completion activity and one or more Listening Completion activities.

*Note that the practice activities in the Booster are not intended to test student achievement after each unit. Complete Achievement Tests for ***Summit*** can be found in the ***Summit*** ActiveTeach.

UNIT 1

READING COMPLETION

Read the selection. Choose the word or phrase that best completes each statement.

Gender Roles

Until recently in the developed world, most married couples **(1)** ..... traditional roles, with the husband working outside the home and the wife taking care of the children and the house. Although many families still follow this tradition, those roles have become less iron-clad. A number of factors have contributed to this **(2)** ..... . **(3)** ..... , perhaps as a consequence of feminism, people have begun to believe that one's **(4)** ..... should not dictate one's role. **(5)** ..... , people feel they have "permission" to decide what they want to do in life. It's no longer **(6)** ..... for men to want to be the primary caregiver or homemaker. **(7)** ..... , many women would prefer to enter the working world instead of staying home. **(8)** ..... , a large number of women have achieved advanced academic and professional training, providing them with a significant earning potential.

On the other hand, factors other than personal choice have **(9)** ..... to the fluidity of gender roles. Life has become more expensive and it's **(10)** ..... for a family to exist on only one income, requiring married women to leave the home to earn money to help support the family. **(11)** ..... , the number of two-income households has grown exponentially. And despite the fact that women on average still earn less than men for the same job, their incomes have become an **(12)** ..... component of survival and prosperity in today's world. In similar fashion, a man's decision to stay home may not be voluntary. In the event he has lost his job, his decision to stay home might be one of necessity, not **(13)** ..... .

1	**A** rejected	**B** adopted	**C** gave	**D** needed
2	**A** change	**B** consequence	**C** continuation	**D** conflict
3	**A** Whereas	**B** While	**C** On the one hand	**D** On the other hand
4	**A** parents	**B** income	**C** gender	**D** age
5	**A** Despite this	**B** As a result	**C** Nevertheless	**D** Whereas
6	**A** beneficial	**B** advantageous	**C** harmful	**D** shameful
7	**A** Nevertheless	**B** Despite the fact	**C** By the same token	**D** First
8	**A** On the other hand	**B** Moreover	**C** For example	**D** Finally
9	**A** contradicted	**B** contributed	**C** coincided	**D** donated
10	**A** convenient	**B** difficult	**C** easy	**D** traditional
11	**A** Yet	**B** Even though	**C** Even if	**D** Consequently
12	**A** ordinary	**B** arbitrary	**C** unnecessary	**D** essential
13	**A** need	**B** habit	**C** choice	**D** logic

LISTENING COMPLETION

▶6:27 **You will hear a conversation. Read the paragraph below. Then listen and complete each statement with the word or short phrase you hear in the conversation. Listen a second time to check your work.**

The woman, Diane, is upset because she can't (1) .... Her husband is trying to help her, and he asks her (2) .... she saw it (3) .... She remembers that she used it (4) .... her friend Mark when she was (5) .... Her husband asks if she had been (6) .... when she texted Mark. Diane wants to know why that question is relevant, and her husband says that even though it's (7) .... to text while driving, the main reason he asked was to help her figure out when she (8) .... That question helps Diane remember that she had been downstairs (9) .... when she texted and that she had stuck (10) .... in the grocery bag.

UNIT 2

READING COMPLETION

Read the selection. Choose the word or phrase that best completes each statement.

Where Values Come From

All of us live by a set of principles or beliefs that guide our actions and help us develop a sense of what is morally acceptable **(1)** ..... what is unacceptable behavior. But where do our values come from? According to psychologists, they develop throughout our lives and **(2)** ..... from a variety of sources, such as family, school, religious upbringing, the places we work in, **(3)** ..... as the media and music we watch and listen to.

For example, most of us learn from our parents to **(4)** ..... between right and wrong. When they read to us or tell us children's stories, we **(5)** ..... moral lessons about the consequences of good and bad behavior. **(6)** ..... we make mistakes or when we don't tell the truth, our parents correct us. Moreover, we learn from our parents' actions. Children **(7)** ..... how their parents relate to each other and handle social situations, and they always notice whether their parents are truthful or not.

(8) ..... , we are strongly affected by the views of our peers. Our friends, colleagues, and acquaintances "categorize" the people we know or who we hear about on the news—for example, who is unfriendly, who is generous, which politicians or celebrities are honest. Many people also believe their moral principles can be **(9)** ..... to their religious upbringing. Religion can provide a clear set of guidelines to live by that make it easier to distinguish between right and wrong.

	A	B	C	D
1	**A** between	**B** from	**C** to	**D** about
2	**A** originate	**B** learn	**C** match	**D** populate
3	**A** known	**B** such	**C** as well	**D** as far
4	**A** activate	**B** distinguish	**C** enter	**D** educate
5	**A** absorb	**B** calculate	**C** inspire	**D** encourage
6	**A** Therefore	**B** Although	**C** Even if	**D** When
7	**A** observe	**B** disagree	**C** ignore	**D** compete
8	**A** Consequently	**B** As a result	**C** For instance	**D** Similarly
9	**A** described	**B** contributed	**C** attributed	**D** celebrated

LISTENING COMPLETION

▶6:28 **You will hear part of a report. Read the paragraph below. Then listen and complete each statement with the word or short phrase you hear in the report. Listen a second time to check your work.**

In the report, the speaker notes that celebrity philanthropists get lots of attention but also have their (1) .... For example, an aid worker complains that bringing celebrities in to do humanitarian work is more (2) .... it's worth. Why? Because celebrity philanthropists can be (3) .... and demanding. They also often do little to (4) .... the people they came to help. On the other hand, supporters note that some celebrity philanthropists (5) .... way and don't ask for special (6) .... Another criticism of celebrity philanthropists, however, is that they sometimes spread a (7) .... that places like Africa are hopeless and (8) .... Finally, some critics say celebrities (9) .... local humanitarian efforts and provide increased opportunities for (10) ....

UNIT 3

READING COMPLETION

Read the selection. Choose the word or phrase that best completes each statement.

Avoiding Hearing Loss

Hearing plays a crucial role in all aspects of communication and learning. **(1)** ..... does even a small amount of hearing loss have a profound, negative effect on language development and comprehension, it **(2)** ..... affects the classroom learning of students who have difficulty hearing. **(3)** ..... deafness that occurs at birth or because of disease or injury, permanent **(4)** ..... to hearing can result from excessive exposure to noise. In fact, millions of people **(5)** ..... from this sort of hearing loss, called "noise-induced hearing loss." It is **(6)** ..... by damage to structures and / or nerve fibers in the inner ear. It can result from a one-time exposure to a very loud sound or from listening to loud sounds over an extended period of time. Unfortunately, noise-induced hearing loss cannot be medically or surgically **(7)** ..... .

So how can noise-induced hearing loss be **(8)** ..... ? In some cases it's impossible to avoid the **(9)** ..... exposure to one very loud sound, and some work environments are noisy. Nevertheless, there are many cases in which people can avoid voluntary exposure to loud sounds, and they **(10)** ..... . What are some steps anyone can take? Most importantly, identify the **(11)** ..... of loud sounds, such as lawnmowers, power tools, and music in your life. Next, adopt behaviors to protect hearing, such as avoiding or **(12)** ..... exposure to the loud sounds as much as you can. After that, make it a practice to automatically turn down the volume of music systems. Finally, when it's not feasible to avoid or **(13)** ..... loud sounds, use hearing protection devices. Such devices can reduce the noise to a safe level.

	A	B	C	D
1	**A** Even though	**B** Not only	**C** If only	**D** Therefore
2	**A** yet	**B** in spite of this	**C** even if	**D** also
3	**A** Whenever	**B** Whereas	**C** Before	**D** Unlike
4	**A** aid	**B** damage	**C** benefits	**D** symptoms
5	**A** enjoy	**B** are helped	**C** result	**D** suffer
6	**A** aided	**B** caused	**C** benefitted	**D** cured
7	**A** caused	**B** corrected	**C** heard	**D** possible
8	**A** improved	**B** prevented	**C** treated	**D** confirmed
9	**A** fortunate	**B** accidental	**C** intentional	**D** obvious
10	**A** can	**B** might	**C** should	**D** do not
11	**A** effects	**B** sources	**C** problems	**D** consequences
12	**A** limiting	**B** combining	**C** making	**D** causing
13	**A** increase	**B** hope for	**C** create	**D** reduce

LISTENING COMPLETION

▶ 6:29 You will hear a report. Read the paragraph below. Then listen and complete each statement with the word or short phrase you hear in the report. Listen a second time to check your work.

Seol Ik Soo, a Korean (1) .... who was a passenger on a flight returning (2) .... South Korea (3) .... China, was daydreaming about his wife as the plane prepared (4) .... He and his wife had been married only (5) .... before and this was the first time they had been (6) .... Suddenly, he saw a ball of (7) .... in the cabin of the plane and the plane (8) .... Luckily, Seol escaped through a hole in the crashed plane. From outside of the plane he could hear other passengers calling (9) .... Instead of running away, Seol went back in to rescue others. No one knows exactly how many passengers Seol managed to carry out of the plane. There may have been (10) .... ten. After it was all over, Seol was asked how he had managed to behave so heroically and he responded that he's sure he couldn't have done it in his (11) ....

UNIT 4

READING COMPLETION

Read the selection. Choose the word or phrase that best completes each statement.

Friendship

In the words of a famous song, friendship is "like a bridge over troubled water." In other words, you can always count on your friends' support when you need it the **(1)** ..... . Friends can tell when you're feeling **(2)** ..... , and they know whether or not you want to talk about it. They are thoughtful when it comes to your well-being, and they can **(3)** ..... according to your needs.

The truth is we need our friends to be dependable—through thick and thin. **(4)** ..... constantly trying to change you, good friends accept you as you are. And good friends roll with the punches. They get it that inside you're a good person with flaws, and that those shortcomings are part of who you are. **(5)** ..... , they know you make mistakes, and they forgive you for them, knowing you'll try to do better next time. And when people criticize you, friends stick up for you because even **(6)** ..... you're being difficult, friends are patient.

While you and your friends may have disagreements, you **(7)** ..... respect each other's opinions. Above all, you need to know that you can **(8)** ..... your friends with your secrets. If there's a problem between you, a friend will talk to you **(9)** ..... and not gossip about you with others. We can always count on our friends to be honest with us when others aren't. Friends don't keep things bottled up inside. Whenever there's an **(10)** ..... , they work things out together and move on.

1	**A** heaviest	**B** most	**C** least	**D** nearest
2	**A** ready	**B** cold	**C** energetic	**D** blue
3	**A** criticize	**B** argue	**C** adjust	**D** learn
4	**A** Rather than	**B** Whereas	**C** Despite	**D** Before
5	**A** Moreover	**B** Otherwise	**C** Whether or not	**D** Unfortunately
6	**A** despite	**B** especially	**C** when	**D** so
7	**A** should	**B** never	**C** don't	**D** might
8	**A** help	**B** save	**C** trust	**D** lend
9	**A** formally	**B** casually	**C** importantly	**D** directly
10	**A** accident	**B** issue	**C** attribute	**D** examination

LISTENING COMPLETION

A ▶6:30 **You will hear a description. Read the paragraph below. Then listen and complete each statement with the word or short phrase you hear in the description. Listen a second time to check your work.**

The woman says she sometimes feels (1) .... because she's so (2) .... She says that when she puts things away, she then can't (3) .... She feels embarrassed to (4) .... because there's such a mess. So she asked her friend Alicia for help because Alicia's so (5) .... Alicia helped her (6) .... all her stuff to decide what was important and what she could (7) ....

B ▶6:31 **You will hear a description. Read the paragraph below. Then listen and complete each statement with the word or short phrase you hear in the description. Listen a second time to check your work.**

The woman is concerned about what she calls a problem with her (8) .... It's not a problem at (9) .... , but she worries when she gets really angry at her (10) .... and starts (11) .... at them. She believes that, after a bad day at work, she's just (12) .... it out on them. As a result, she took a workshop on (13) .... , where she learned that it's important to let off a little steam. So she took up (14) .... three days a week. When she feels angry, exercising helps her (15) .... what's making her mad.

UNIT 5

READING COMPLETION

Read the selection. Choose the word or phrase that best completes each statement.

Laughter Yoga

The principle of Laughter Yoga is that you cannot be physically stressed and mentally relaxed at the same time. **(1)** ..... most forms of Yoga include body positions and exercises, Laughter Yoga is based on the physical activity of laughing, which relaxes the body and mind. Proponents of Laughter Yoga **(2)** ..... that it permits us to be more aware of the present **(3)** ..... dwelling on the past or worrying about the future. In short, it enables us to simply *be*.

Some **(4)** ..... that Laughter Yoga can be considered a new form of exercise. **(5)** ..... its proponents, it's a kind of internal jogging. Anyone can do it because, they say, everybody knows how to laugh. It is not necessary to tell jokes, have a sense of **(6)** ..... , or be happy in order to laugh. In fact, practitioners of Laughter Yoga are invited to "laugh for no reason," faking the laughter until it becomes real. It is **(7)** ..... that the physical action of laughing brings oxygen and certain body chemicals such as hormones to the body and the brain, thus fostering **(8)** ..... feelings and improving interpersonal skills. **(9)** ..... Laughter Yoga is practiced in groups, people leave each session laughing and feeling **(10)** ..... to each other. Believers in Laughter Yoga **(11)** ..... contend it can contribute to world peace. They say, "World peace first starts inside every one of us. We don't laugh because we are happy. We are happy because we laugh."

	A	B	C	D
1	**A** Until	**B** While	**C** Whether	**D** If
2	**A** continue	**B** complain	**C** assert	**D** admit
3	**A** in addition to	**B** instead of	**C** in favor of	**D** along with
4	**A** tell	**B** ask	**C** claim	**D** wonder
5	**A** Even if	**B** Whenever	**C** Although	**D** According to
6	**A** anger	**B** humor	**C** happiness	**D** knowledge
7	**A** argued	**B** disputed	**C** required	**D** intended
8	**A** negative	**B** hopeless	**C** lucky	**D** positive
9	**A** Since	**B** All the same	**C** Even if	**D** Until
10	**A** separate	**B** connected	**C** different	**D** annoyed
11	**A** however	**B** nevertheless	**C** therefore	**D** besides

LISTENING COMPLETION

▶6:32 **You will hear a story. Read the paragraph below. Then listen and complete each statement with the word or short phrase you hear in the story. Listen a second time to check your work.**

The woman tells a story about her friend Mark, who loves to (1) .... Mark decided to play a joke on his friend John, who was very (2) .... and was always looking for (3) .... One day, Mark spoke to (4) .... of the Bargain Burger restaurant and asked her if she would (5) .... two very large burgers. The manager said "Sure," and Mark paid her for them (6) .... Mark explained that he would bring (7) .... for lunch and that the manager should (8) .... the huge burgers and put the regular low price on the check. When Mark and John finished eating, (9) .... and John was pleasantly surprised at the low price of the burgers. So the (10) .... John invited a couple of his friends to Bargain Burger for the huge hamburgers. But when the burgers came to the table, they were the ordinary tiny little ones, which made John (11) .... in front of his friends.

THIRD EDITION

SUMMIT 2A

WORKBOOK

JOAN SASLOW
ALLEN ASCHER

UNIT 1

Dreams and Goals

PREVIEW

1 Complete the questionnaire.

FIND YOUR DREAM JOB

Do you have your dream job? If not, and you're thinking of changing careers, or if you're just getting started in the working world, this worksheet can help you focus on what you really want to do. Take time to really think about the questions—your answers could determine your future!

1. If you could study any subject, what would it be?
2. What do you think are your strengths?

3. Ask your friends and family for their opinions about you. What do they think are your strengths?
4. If you suddenly had enough money that you didn't have to earn a living, what would you do with your time?
5. What are your hobbies?

6. Do you like working with people? Or do you prefer to work on your own?
7. Do you prefer working outdoors or inside? In an office, or in a setting where you're not tied to a desk?
8. Think about your friends and family. Does anyone have a job that you'd like to have? What is it?

9. What's a job you'd like to do, but you haven't considered it because you don't have the necessary education or training?

Now look at your answers. Do any skills, jobs, or work settings jump out at you? If not, what do your answers have in common? Is there a skill or an area of study that appears often in your answers? At the very least, your answers should give you food for thought about your ideal career.

2 **Use each expression in a sentence. Use your own ideas.**

a little overkill	keep my fingers crossed
all in all	run of the mill
don't want to take any chances	six of one, half a dozen of the other
I've got my heart set on	wait and see

1. ______________________________
2. ______________________________
3. ______________________________
4. ______________________________
5. ______________________________
6. ______________________________
7. ______________________________
8. ______________________________

3 **WHAT ABOUT YOU? Answer the questions.**

1. Have you ever considered changing your career or course of study? Why or why not?

   ____

2. What job do you see yourself doing in ten years?

   ____

LESSON 1

4 **Read the article. Notice the underlined verbs.**

The Brooklyn Bridge: *A Story of Triumph*

Already an accomplished bridge designer in the mid-1800s, John Roebling wanted to pursue his greatest challenge yet: building a bridge connecting Manhattan with rapidly growing Brooklyn. However, this would be no ordinary bridge. It would span the East River, which flows in more than one direction and can be navigated by ships. The bridge would have to be tall enough for ships to pass under. Roebling's idea was not well received. No one had done anything like it, and experts claimed it was impossible. Many people even doubted the necessity of the bridge.

But Roebling persevered, and he drew up plans for the longest suspension bridge in the world at that time. In 1869 construction began. Roebling had been working on the construction site for only a month when his foot was crushed in a tragic accident. Weeks later he died of complications from the injury. John's son Washington, also an engineer, took over.

Another tragedy soon emphasized the hazards of the project. One stage of construction required workers to go below the river. The effects of the changes in air pressure going from under the river to the surface killed several men and left Washington Roebling paralyzed and unable to speak. But Washington wasn't giving up. He could move one of his fingers a little. He slowly developed a code of communication with his wife Emily by tapping his finger on her arm. With her remarkable assistance, Washington continued to direct the project from his home. Emily took up studies in engineering to better understand Washington's plans. For thirteen years she oversaw work at the construction site.

Even before its opening on May 24, 1883, the bridge had come to symbolize triumph and ingenuity. Today the Brooklyn Bridge remains a tribute to perseverance and determination.

The Brooklyn Bridge connects the boroughs of Manhattan and Brooklyn in New York City.

Now complete the chart. Write the underlined verbs in the correct categories.

Simple past	Past perfect	Past continuous	Past perfect continuous
wanted			

5 **Complete the sentences. Use the correct form of each verb in parentheses.**

1. John Roebling ______ (past perfect continuous) (try) to convince people of his plans for the bridge long before the project ______ (simple past) (become) a reality.
2. John ______ (simple past) (die) before his son Washington ______ (simple past) (take over) as chief engineer.
3. Construction of the bridge ______ (simple past) (lead) to tragedies and triumph in the Roebling family.
4. Emily Roebling ______ (past continuous) (study) engineering while her husband Washington ______ (past continuous) (give) orders for her to carry out.
5. Emily ______ (past perfect continuous) (help) Washington for thirteen years before the bridge ______ (simple past) (be) finally complete.

6 **Circle the action that occurred first in each sentence.**

1. It had been raining for two weeks when the sun finally came out.
2. He was taking a nap when suddenly the alarm clock woke him up.
3. Marianne decided to take action when she got tired of waiting.
4. By the time I found out the news, everyone had heard about it.
5. Mr. Green was waiting for a phone call when someone knocked on the door.
6. They had sent several messages to the company before they got a response.
7. Nancy had been engaged to someone else when she met Jonathan.
8. When the package finally arrived, they'd been expecting it for three weeks.
9. Jennifer saw the ad when she was looking through the newspaper.
10. I had called the office three times before I finally got hold of someone.

7 **Look at the cartoon. Then use appropriate tenses (simple past, past perfect, past continuous, or past perfect continuous) and the verbs in parentheses to complete the sentences. There may be more than one correct answer.**

1. Bud ____________________ (consider) snowboarding down the mountain when Gretchen ____________________ (dare) him to do it.
2. Before Gretchen ____________________ (say) he should do it, Bud ____________________ (think) that snowboarding down the mountain was probably a bad idea.
3. Bud ____________________ (start) to snowboard down the mountain before Gretchen ____________________ (tell) him to stop.
4. When he ____________________ (hear) Gretchen yell, Bud ____________________ (get) really nervous.
5. While he ____________________ (roll) down the mountain, Bud ____________________ (decided) never to snowboard with Gretchen again.

8 **Read the messages on this community website. Then complete the sentences using the phrases from the box.**

four_corners_community.com

Want to change jobs? Check out our website: Careerchange.com

Ballroom dancing beginners' class (for people with no dance experience)
Tuesdays and Thursdays at 7:00 in the Carter Gymnasium

Chef Wanted
The Grand Hotel is looking for a master chef. Training and experience a must. Excellent pay and benefits. Send résumé to Joe.Barker@GrandHotel.com

Having trouble passing your university entrance exams? Not accepted into a program or school? Don't give up! Carlton Test Prep will teach you the exam skills you need to fulfill your dreams. Check us out on the web: carltontestprep.com

Not sure what to do with your life? Talk to a career counselor at FourCornersCareers.com. We can help you make important life choices.

Basic computer classes
6-week course. Our professional instructors will teach you everything you need to know! Morning and evening classes available. ComputersMadeEasy.com

Ballard School of Design is now accepting applications for the fall semester. Submit application and images of your work at Ballarddesign.com

Four Corners Theater Troupe is looking for three actors to join its company for the upcoming season. Prior stage experience a must. Email Emily.Rust@FCTheater.com

accepted into	apply to	enroll in	sign up for	take up
apply for	decide on	rejected by	switch to	

1. People who want to ________ art school can ________ Ballard online.
2. People looking for a job as a chef should email Joe Barker in order to ________ a job.
3. People interested in learning basic computer skills can ________ a computer class.
4. Carlton Test Prep might be helpful for people who've been ________ a school or program because of low test scores.
5. The ballroom dancing class is for people who want to ________ dancing.
6. People who want to ________ a different job should look at careerchange.com.
7. People who can't ________ a career can go to the FourCornersCareers site to ask for advice.
8. Only three actors will be ________ the Four Corners Theater Troupe this season.

9 **Read the e-mail. Underline the verbs in the present perfect. Circle the verbs in the present perfect continuous.**

Dear Mom and Dad,

Well, I've arrived safely, and I'm in my hotel room. I still can't believe I'm here. My dream is finally about to come true! I'm going to skate in the winter Olympic Games! For as long as I can remember I've been dreaming of competing in the Olympics. I've worked so hard for this! I've been training for this day since you took me to my first lesson when I was four years old.

I know you and Dad have given up a lot for me to be here, too. My skating lessons have been expensive, but you have never complained. Everyone has supported me. I know you will all be watching the competition on TV—you've been watching me compete since I first started skating. I hope that I do well so I can make you proud.

Your loving daughter, Tracy

10 **Complete the e-mail response from Tracy's mother. Use the present perfect continuous for uncompleted actions, except with stative verbs. Use the present perfect for completed actions.**

Dear Tracy,

Your father and I are so proud of you! Since you were a little girl, I ___have known___ (1. know) that you would become a great skater one day. You ______________ (2. talk) about skating in the Olympics since we bought you your first pair of ice skates. I know that sometimes ice skating ______________ (3. seem) like a lot of work. Injuries ______________ (4. make) you slow down a few times, but you ______________ (5. not forget) your goal. And now your dream is finally a reality. We ______________ (6. watch) you grow from a child to the amazing athlete and beautiful person that you are today. Over the years, we ______________ (7. see) you win, lose, and try again. No matter what happens in the next two weeks, we'll be proud of you just like we ______________ (8. be) for so many years.

Love always, Mom

11 **Mark grammatically correct sentences with a checkmark. Mark incorrect sentences with an ✗. Rewrite the incorrect sentences using appropriate verb forms.**

1. ☒ I've just been enrolling in the pre-med program at the university.
   I've just enrolled in the pre-med program at the university.
2. ☐ I've had an interest in sculpture for many years.
   ____
3. ☐ Have you been accepted by any schools yet?
   ____
4. ☐ How many jobs has he been applying for?
   ____
5. ☐ My daughter's been visiting a lot of universities lately.
   ____
6. ☐ Have you ever been thinking of a career change?
   ____
7. ☐ The group has been working on the project for over a year.
   ____
8. ☐ I haven't been deciding on a career yet.
   ____
9. ☐ I've been owning my car for a year now.
   ____
10. ☐ We've thought about moving, but we really like our neighborhood.
    ____
11. ☐ The International Red Cross has helped people all over the world.
    ____
12. ☐ I've traveled around Italy for the past few months, and I'm loving every minute of it.
    ____

12 **WHAT ABOUT YOU? Complete the questions with the present perfect or present perfect continuous. Then answer the questions.**

1. What is one accomplishment that you ________________ (achieve) in the past?
   ____
2. What is one activity that you ________________ (do) for a few years?
   ____
3. What is one thing or activity that you ________________ (be) interested in for a long time?
   ____
4. What's one thing that you ________________ (try) to do for a while?
   ____
5. What's one important lesson that you ________________ (learn) in your life?
   ____

13 **Complete the paragraph using the words from the box.**

ambitious	fulfill	put off	unrealistic
achievable	pursuing	set a goal	

When I was 11 years old, I went snorkeling in the ocean for the first time. That was when I knew that I wanted to be a marine biologist. It was a(n) ______ (1.) goal for an 11-year-old, but I knew that it was ______ (2.) if I worked hard. Since then, I've been ______ (3.) my dream. In high school I took as many science classes as I could. I studied hard and got good grades. It helped that I enjoyed what I was studying. My parents didn't make a lot of money, but I knew it wasn't ______ (4.) to think I could get a scholarship to a good university. I did, and, in four years, I got my undergraduate degree in marine biology. I had to ______ (5.) graduate school for a couple of years, but I got an interesting job as a laboratory assistant, so it wasn't so bad. Finally, I was accepted into the graduate program at the university that was my first choice. Now, three years later, I am about to ______ (6.) my dream and graduate with my doctorate in marine biology! Anything is possible if you ______ (7.) and work diligently towards achieving it.

14 **Answer the questions.**

1. What was one of your childhood dreams? ______
2. Was that childhood dream realistic? Why or why not? ______
3. Is it still a dream of yours? If so, what are you doing to pursue your dream? If not, what has changed? ______
4. If you live with another family member or a roommate, how do you share responsibilities? ______
5. What is something that you've been putting off? Why? ______
6. Do you think that it's important for children to have one stay-at-home parent? Explain. ______
7. What differences do you think there might be between how children with a stay-at-home father are raised and how those with a stay-at-home mother are raised? ______

LESSON 4

15 **Read the article.**

Interviewing for Success

You sent your résumé to several employers, and you got an interview! Congratulations—that's an important step toward landing your dream job. Now you need to prepare for the interview. There's no way to know exactly what questions the interviewer will ask, but there's a good chance that you'll be asked at least some of the questions that follow. Preparing a basic answer to each of them will, first of all, keep you from racking your brain for an answer at the last minute. Even more importantly, it will give you an extra measure of confidence. And a confident candidate is more likely to land the job.

So, let's take a look at some of the typical questions interviewers often ask.

1. Tell me a little bit about yourself.
This seems like a pretty easy question to answer, but you need to give this one some thought and tailor your answer to the job for which you are interviewing. The interviewer doesn't want to know everything about you; he or she is interested in the qualities that will make you the best person for the job. So research the position and prepare a two- to three-minute answer that highlights what it is about you that makes you the best candidate. Remember: this will probably be the first question you are asked, so make your answer a good one so you make a good first impression.

2. Why are you looking for a new job?
This question will almost certainly come up in your interview, so it's best to be prepared for it. If you are a student looking for your first job, the answer is easy. But if you are currently employed, you'll need to explain why you want to leave your current position for a new one. The best thing to do is to highlight the positive aspects of the new job, rather than dwell on any negative aspects of the old job. For example, "I've learned a lot in my current position, but I'm ready for new challenges, which I think I can find at your company." Remember: the key is to avoid being negative about your current job, while telling the truth about why you want to move on.

3. What would you say are your greatest strengths?
This is another question that you will likely be asked, along with its inverse: What is your greatest weakness? Let's start with your strengths. It's hard for many people to talk about their strengths, because it feels like bragging. Start by thinking about which of your strengths and qualifications would be valuable in the position for which you're applying. Those are the ones you want to focus on. Practice talking about them in a way that feels comfortable for you. Remember to provide examples of specific times you have demonstrated each strength.
And now for what might be the harder question:

4. What is your greatest weakness?
You may be thinking, "I don't want to say anything negative about myself; if I do they won't want to hire me." The key when answering this question is to be honest but positive. You should choose a real weakness, but one which you are working to overcome. You want the interviewer to see that you are not afraid to admit that you can improve. For example, "I am not as proficient at [computer programming] as I would like to be, but I have enrolled in an evening training program, and I can see improvement already."

Last but not least, as you're thinking about your answers to these common interview questions, remember to be yourself. Your answers should be truthful and should reflect your qualifications in a way that feels natural to you. Good luck!

Now answer the questions.

1. Why is it important to prepare answers to commonly asked questions before an interview?
____
2. When an interviewer asks you to tell him or her about yourself, what type of information should you include? _______________
____
3. What should you NOT do when explaining why you are looking for a new position?
____
4. What problem might some people have when asked about their greatest strengths?
____
5. In addition to listing your strengths, what should you do? _______________
____
6. What should be your goal when answering the question, "What is your greatest weakness?"
____

16 **Now imagine that you are interviewing for your dream job. Answer the questions.**

1. Tell me a little bit about yourself. _______________
____
____
2. Why are you looking for a new job? _______________
____
____
3. What are your greatest strengths? _______________
____
____
4. What is your greatest weakness? _______________
____
____

17 **WHAT ABOUT YOU? Complete the sentences.**

1. I have experience _______________.
2. I want to get experience in _______________ so I can _______________.
3. I need to get training in _______________ if I want to _______________.
4. I have a degree or certificate in _______________.
5. I hope to get certified in _______________ so I can _______________.
____

GRAMMAR BOOSTER

A **Choose the correct answer to complete each sentence.**

1. She _____ to work when her car suddenly started smoking.
   a. would drive   b. has driven   c. was driving
2. I _____ Turkish food a few times, and I really like it.
   a. used to eat   b. have eaten   c. was going to
3. We _____ soccer last weekend.
   a. would play   b. used to play   c. played
4. They _____ vegetables at the market this morning, but it was closed.
   a. would buy   b. bought   c. were going to buy
5. I _____ you yesterday, but I didn't have time.
   a. had called   b. was going to call   c. was calling
6. Everyone _____ at the office at 8:30 this morning.
   a. was   b. used to be   c. has been
7. The workers _____ painting the house before the storm started.
   a. have finished   b. used to finish   c. had finished
8. I always knew I _____ a house near the beach one day.
   a. would buy   b. bought   c. had bought
9. Tom _____ meat, but now he doesn't.
   a. was going to eat   b. used to eat   c. was eating

B **Cross out the word or phrase that does not correctly complete each sentence.**

1. As a child, Betsy **used to bother / bothered / was bothering** her younger brothers a lot.
2. The team **had been working / used to work / had worked** on the project for months before it was finally finished.
3. I **had walked / walked / was walking** there twice before I learned I could take a bus.
4. The secretary **had left / left / was leaving** a message for Mr. Reynolds on Monday evening before she went home.
5. She thought that she **would see / had seen / had been seeing** that movie by herself.
6. She **used to study / has studied / studied** all the time when she was a student.
7. They **were waiting / had been waiting / waited** for over an hour before their table was ready.

C **WHAT ABOUT YOU? Answer the questions.**

1. What did you do yesterday evening?

   ____

2. What is something that you used to do when you were a child?

   ____

3. What is something that you thought you would have done by the age that you are now?

____

4. What is something that you've done a few times in the past year?

____

D **Read each sentence. Write C if the sentence is grammatically correct or I if it is incorrect. Fix the incorrect sentences.**

1. __I__ ~~I'm understand~~ I understand that this is a difficult time for many employees.
2. _____ The secretary remembers that she left the file on Mr. Johnson's desk.
3. _____ Are you having a few minutes to discuss our plans for the project?
4. _____ John is knowing your brother because they went to school together.
5. _____ I'm going to visit my travel agent today. I'm thinking of taking a vacation.
6. _____ This bag is really heavy. How much is it weighing?
7. _____ We're having steak for dinner. Would you like to join us?
8. _____ I'm believing that it's important for family members to live near one another.
9. _____ Mary is looking at photographs of her wedding.
10. _____ This sauce is tasting a little too salty.

E **Complete the sentences with the simple present or present continuous form of the verbs in parentheses.**

1. A: Are these photos of your grandchildren?
   B: Yes. My oldest daughter ____________ (have) two sons, and she ____________ (have) another one in the spring.
2. A: I read that the average newborn baby ____________ (weigh) between three and four kilograms.
   B: How heavy is Hannah?
   A: I don't know. The nurse ____________ (weigh) her now.
3. A: I ____________ (see) Julia in the hallway. Want me to get that file from her?
   B: No, don't bother. I ____________ (see) her after lunch. We have a meeting at two o'clock.
4. A: The food here is delicious. They ____________ (have) a lot of great seafood dishes on the menu.
   B: I don't feel like seafood tonight. I ____________ (have) a salad.
5. A: My parents ____________ (think) I watch too much TV.
   B: Mine do, too. They ____________ (think) about getting rid of our television.
6. A: Did Anne think this sauce ____________ (taste) different?
   B: I'm not sure. She ____________ (taste) it now.
7. A: What are you doing?
   B: I ____________ (look) at a photo of my brother's new house. It ____________ (look) beautiful!

WRITING A formal cover letter

A **PREWRITING: TREE DIAGRAM** Look at the tree diagram below. On a separate sheet of paper, create your own tree diagram about your experience, knowledge, training, and abilities. Write ideas in under each section and expand each new idea.

JEFF BROCKMAN

Experience
- wrote articles for local newspaper
- wrote weekly column for college newspaper
- on editorial board of college newspaper

Knowledge
- design newspaper layout with computer software
- some Japanese
- German

Training
- attended writers' workshop
- degree in journalism from Loyalton University

Abilities
- type 55 words per minute
- work well in groups
- work independently

B **WRITING** Most often you will write a cover letter to apply for a specific job. But suppose you wanted to work for the company DreamTECH (or for another real or imaginary company), but did not yet know of a specific job posting. On a separate sheet of paper, write a cover letter to send your résumé to the Director of Human Resources at that company. Use some of your ideas from the idea cluster. Use the cover letter on Student's Book page 12 as a model.

C **SELF-CHECK**

- ☐ Does my letter have any spelling, punctuation, or typographical errors?
- ☐ Did I use formal letter writing conventions?
- ☐ Did I tell the employer the purpose of my letter?
- ☐ Did I say why I think I would be a good candidate?
- ☐ Did I tell the employer how to contact me for follow-up?

UNIT 2 Character and Responsibility

PREVIEW

1 **Answer the questions. Use true information or make up fictitious answers.**

1. Have you ever made a serious mistake at work or school? Explain.

____

____

____

2. Did you admit your mistake? Explain.

____

____

____

3. Have you ever forgotten to finish an assignment for work or school? What happened? ____

____

____

4. Have you ever broken or lost something you had borrowed? What happened? ____

____

____

5. Have you ever broken a promise? Explain.

____

____

6. Has anyone ever told you a lie? What did you do?

____

____

7. Have you ever told a lie? Did you have a good reason? Explain.

____

____

____

8. Have you ever damaged someone else's car? What happened?

____

____

____

2 **Look at the picture. Then write a statement describing the attitude or action of each child. Use phrases from the box. There may be more than one correct answer.**

admit making a mistake	express regret	make up for	take responsibility for
avoid taking responsibility for	make up an excuse	shift the blame to	

1. (Charlie) ______________________________
2. (Sally) ______________________________
3. (Billy) ______________________________
4. (Jane) ______________________________
5. (John) ______________________________

3 **Complete the conversations with expressions from the box.**

couldn't help myself	make it up to	owned up to
let things get out of hand	making fun of	that's not the worst of it

1. **A:** Hello?
   B: Hi Jamie, this is Kelly. I wanted to apologize for ______________________ your outfit.
   A: Oh Kelly, that's ok. I didn't take it seriously.

2. **A:** What's wrong, Jen?
   B: I messed up big time. I forgot to hand in my final assignment.
   A: Well, the semester just ended. Can you email the professor and ask if you can hand it in today?
   B: But ______________________. I haven't even finished it!

3. **A:** Who ate all the cake? Billy?
   B: I'm sorry, Mom. I ______________________. It was so good!
   A: Billy, what am I going to do with you? Well, at least you ______________________ it and didn't try to shift the blame to the dog!

4. A: Brenda, I'm so sorry I forgot your birthday!
   B: Oh Amy, that's ok. At our age, birthdays aren't such a big deal.
   A: Still, let me ______________________ you. Can I buy you dinner this week?
   B: Well, you certainly don't need to, but yes, let's go out to dinner. It will be nice to catch up.

5. A: How was the party at the beach last night?
   B: It was great fun. But we may have ______________________.
   A: What do you mean?
   B: Some people were swimming in the dark. That doesn't seem like a good idea now.

LESSON 1

4 **Read the article. Then read each statement and check True or False.**

LIE DETECTOR

How to tell if someone is lying to you

People lie for a variety of reasons, and everyone lies sometimes. But has there ever been a time when you wondered if someone was lying to you? Here are a few behaviors that may indicate that the person is lying.

People who are lying often...

- avoid making eye contact.
- touch their face, throat, and mouth. Liars are not likely to touch their chest or heart with an open hand.
- turn away from the person to whom they are lying.
- place objects such as a book or coffee cup between themselves and the person to whom they are lying.
- give answers which are longer than necessary. For example, if you ask, "Did you take the money?" a liar might say, "No, I did not take the money," instead of just, "No."
- give more details than are needed. Liars are uncomfortable when there is silence or a pause in the conversation.

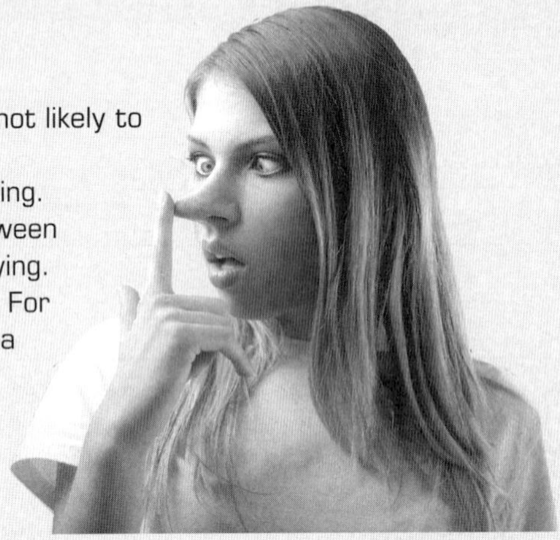

Important! These are only indications that a person is lying. A person who is lying might not show these signs, or a person who shows some of these signs might actually be telling the truth.

	True	False
1. If the person with whom you're speaking avoids looking you in the eye, then he or she is certainly lying.	☐	☐
2. When people lie, they often turn their bodies away from the person to whom they are speaking.	☐	☐
3. When a person tells a lie to make an excuse, he or she might talk more than is necessary.	☐	☐
4. If a person touches his or her chest while talking, then he or she is probably lying.	☐	☐

5 **CHALLENGE** **Look at the pictures. Complete each conversation by creating a lie for the second speaker. Then answer each question. Decide whether the person is lying to avoid hurting someone else's feelings or to make an excuse.**

1. Why is the girl lying?

   She's making an excuse to avoid being punished by her father.

2. Why is the worker lying?

   ____

   ____

3. Why is the boy lying?

   ____

   ____

4. Why is the woman lying?

   ____

   ____

6 **WHAT ABOUT YOU?** **What would you say in each situation? Would you lie? Explain your answers.**

Situation	Your response
You go to a friend's house for dinner, and he serves fish. He says, "I hope you like seafood." You hate it.	
A co-worker is wearing a new outfit. She asks if you like it. You think it's inappropriate for the office.	
A neighbor who you don't really like invites you to a party. You don't have any plans for that evening but you don't want to go.	
You forgot to do your homework. Your teacher asks why you didn't complete the assignment.	

7 **Complete the statements with who, whom, which, when, where, or whose.**

1. A liar is someone ________________ doesn't tell the truth.
2. There are very few people, if any, ________________ never lie.
3. Most people feel at least a little bit uncomfortable ________________ they lie.
4. Is there anyone to ________________ most people never lie?
5. There are times ________________ telling a lie can keep you out of trouble.
6. People ________________ lie a lot are often people ________________ reputations aren't very good.
7. Lying to avoid hurting someone's feelings is a situation in ________________ people often find themselves.
8. Work is one place ________________ people sometimes lie to avoid getting in trouble.

"A person who lies for you will lie against you."
—Bosnian proverb

8 **WHAT ABOUT YOU?** **Complete the statements with your own words and who, whom, that, when, where, or whose.**

1. ________________ is a person ________________ I'd like to meet.
2. ________________ is the city ________________ I was born.
3. ________________ is a holiday ________________ many families get together.
4. ________________ and ________________ are things ________________ interest me.
5. ________________ is someone ________________ ideas I find interesting.
6. ________________ is a person with ________________ I enjoy spending time.

LESSON 2

9 **Complete each sentence with a comment clause with which. Use the ideas in the box.**

I don't think it's necessary.	I thought it was unfair.
~~I feel awful about it.~~	It was ok, since I was busy anyway.
I find it annoying.	It was very sweet of him.

1. I forgot my aunt's birthday, *which I feel awful about.*
2. Jared still hasn't returned the book I lent him last year, ________________.
3. Sarah was half an hour late to our meeting, ________________.
4. Tommy helped his sister clean up her mess, ________________.
5. Stu wants to replace the vase that he broke, ________________.
6. There was material on the test that we hadn't studied in class, ________________.

10 **Read the letter to an advice columnist. Then read the columnist's response.**

Dear Anita,

I have a friend who frequently asks to borrow things from me. Since she's one of my best friends, I always say yes. But she doesn't take good care of my things. Last month I lent her a book and when she gave it back, the pages were ripped. When I asked her about it, she claimed that the pages were ripped when I loaned it to her, which wasn't true—it was a brand new book! Another time I let her use one of my favorite handbags. I don't know how, but she got a hole in it. That time she said she was sorry, and she admitted that it was her fault. Unfortunately, she still hasn't given me any money for it, which bothers me. Once she borrowed a pair of my shoes, and her dog chewed them. But she said it wasn't her fault—it was her sister's fault because her sister let the dog into her bedroom!

I want to keep my friend, but I can't continue with the way things are going.

Please help!
Christina

Dear Christina,

You sound like a very good and forgiving friend. But it also sounds like you might be a pushover. I know it can be hard to talk openly about a friend's behavior when it bothers you. But it's important. You need to learn to say no, and your friend needs to learn to take responsibility. Next time, before you lend your friend something, tell her that you want it back in the same condition. Tell her you'll expect her to take responsibility for any damage, which is only fair. That way, you explain your expectations and make a plan if she doesn't meet them. Good luck!

Sincerely,
Anita

Now choose the correct answer to complete each statement.

1. Christina's friend doesn't often ____.
   a. borrow things from Christina
   b. ruin things
   c. take responsibility for her mistakes
2. Christina's friend ____ the ripped pages in the book.
   a. felt awful about
   b. made an excuse about
   c. took responsibility for

3. When Christina's friend damaged the handbag, she ____.
   a. made up an excuse
   b. admitted making a mistake
   c. shifted the blame to someone else

4. After Christina's friend returned the damaged bag, she didn't ____.
   a. make it up to Christina
   b. know about the problem with the bag
   c. admit that the hole in the bag was her fault

5. When the dog ruined Christina's shoes, her friend ____.
   a. shifted the blame to someone else
   b. took responsibility
   c. made it up to Christina

6. Anita thinks that Christina should ____.
   a. express regret
   b. make excuses for her friend
   c. make her friend take responsibility

11 **WHAT ABOUT YOU? Read the following situation. If you were involved in this situation, would you take responsibility for the accident, avoid responsibility, or shift the blame to someone else? Explain your answer.**

You're a college student and, to earn money for school, you have started working a part-time job at a restaurant. On your first day on the job, the manager gives you the keys to the delivery van and asks you to pick up some cakes from a bakery down the street. You have never driven a large van before but, because it's your first day, you are afraid of saying no to your new boss. When driving the van to pick up the cakes, you notice a large, luxury car parked on the street. The car has been parked too far from the sidewalk and sticks out into the street. When you pass the parked car, you accidentally hit it. You stop the van and check the damage, and you notice that the side mirror of the parked car is broken, but that the van has only a few paint scrapes. The street is empty and nobody saw the accident.

____

____

____

____

____

12 **Read the article.**

JOURNAL OF HUMAN BEHAVIOR

The Trolley Problem

Does our behavior reflect our character and our values? Most people would answer yes to this question. Many researchers have studied what people do (or say they would do) when faced with having to choose between two opposing values. One classic dilemma is known as the "Trolley Problem."

Imagine this scenario: You are standing next to a track on which a runaway trolley car is speeding straight toward five people tied to the track. They are sure to die in seconds. However, you can save the five people by simply flipping a switch, which will divert the trolley onto another track, saving the five people. However, there is one person tied to that second track, and he will surely be killed as a result of your action. What do you do?

This ethical dilemma was originally developed in 1967 by moral philosopher Philippa Foot and has been used since then by people studying human ethics, morals, and values. As it turns out, a majority of people would pull the lever and sacrifice the one person, thereby saving the five people. This seems to be a relatively clear mathematical equation for most people: one person's death is outweighed by the fact that five people were saved as a result.

Things get a little more confusing when you add a slightly different scenario to the problem. This version was developed in the 1980s by philosopher Judith Jarvis Thomson. In Thomson's version, you are again standing near the tracks, the trolley is again hurtling toward the five people tied to the tracks, and they are again certain to die. This time, there is no switch and no second track. However, there is a fat man standing next to the track. If you push the man onto the track, his body will stop the train. He will be killed, but the five people will be saved. Mathematically, this is the same calculation as in the first version of the dilemma. But the difference: the majority of people would NOT push the fat man.

Why the difference? The mathematical equation is the same: five people's lives versus one person's life. Researchers have been trying to solve this question for decades. Studies have shown that when people think about actually pushing someone to his death, areas of the brain that deal with emotion are active. However, when they think about flipping the switch, areas of the brain associated with higher reasoning are active. This may provide some clue as to why the responses to these two similar versions of the dilemma are so markedly different. What do you think?

VOLUME 27, ISSUE 5

Now answer the questions.

1. Restate the two versions of the Trolley Problem in your own words.

____

____

____

____

2. Do you think the two versions of the problem are morally or ethically different? Explain.

3. Why do you think most people would pull the lever but not push the man?

13 **WHAT ABOUT YOU? What would you do if faced with the first version of the Trolley Problem? What about the second version? Explain.**

LESSON 4

14 **Answer the questions.**

1. Have you ever made donations to causes or charities? Explain.

2. Can you think of a famous (or not so famous) philanthropist? Describe what this person does.

3. Do you know of any well-known humanitarians? What do they do?

4. What is one form of activism that you know about? What is the goal of the activists?

15 Read the article.

AN EVERYDAY HERO

Every 56 days, Chip Brady helps save someone's life.

It's not anyone that he knows, and in fact he's probably never even met any of the people he's helped. Chip is a voluntary blood donor. For him, giving blood is a deep, purposeful ritual. It's a chance to express his thankfulness for his own good health, and it's an opportunity to help people in his community. "This is one way that I can truly make a difference in people's lives," he says.

It started when Chip signed up for his company's annual blood drive. He was surprised at how quick and easy the donation was. He also recalls a great sense of contentment and pride at being able to help others. He always knew that giving blood was important, but he didn't expect how great it would make him feel. "Every time I give," he says, "I get this incredible sense of satisfaction because I know that I'm helping someone in the most important way that I can. You never know who might be alive today because of your blood."

Chip admits that sometimes he gets curious about who he's helped. But in the end, he says that he has to be content with just knowing that he's done something good. Chip encourages everyone who can to donate. He wants them to know the joy that comes from helping someone in need.

Now answer the questions.

1. How does Chip Brady make a difference?

____

2. Which of the Vocabulary words on Student's Book page 22 would you use to describe Brady? Explain.

____

____

3. In your own words, explain why Brady donates blood.

____

____

16 **WHAT ABOUT YOU?** Answer the question.

1. Have you ever helped out a stranger? How?

____

2. How do you feel when you help someone?

____

GRAMMAR BOOSTER

A **Mark grammatically correct sentences with a checkmark. Mark incorrect sentences with an ✗. Then correct the incorrect sentences.**

1. ☑ The woman with whom I spoke was very helpful.
2. ☐ The company for whom I worked was very generous.
3. ☐ Now's the time when the truth comes out.
4. ☐ Shirley is a girl that I've known all my life.
5. ☐ The First Avenue Market is one place which I've always gotten fresh fish.
6. ☐ Her ideas are ones what aren't very common.
7. ☐ Is that the teacher which all the students have been talking about?
8. ☐ The palace, whose history can be traced over 500 years, is a historical landmark.
9. ☐ The author who stories won the contest was previously unknown.

B **Complete the sentences. Circle the correct phrase in each pair.**

1. The band has four members, **all of whom** / **both of whom** were born in Melbourne.
2. The guest brought a cake to dinner, **half of which** / **some of whom** was later eaten.
3. There are several rumors going around now, **a little of which** / **none of which** are true.
4. The artist is Alice Flannigan, **most of whom** / **one of whose** favorite colors is blue.
5. The concert includes the compositions of several local musicians, **a little of whom** / **a few of whom** have gone on to record their own albums.
6. I've heard two versions of the story, **none of which** / **neither of which** is very believable.

C **Rewrite each sentence. Reduce the adjective clauses to adjective phrases.**

1. Harry Goldman works for a large company that is located in Osaka.
   Harry Goldman works for a large company located in Osaka.
2. *The Lion, the Witch, and the Wardrobe* was written by C. S. Lewis in 1950.
   ____
3. Those photos, which prove the innocence of the defendant, have been turned over to the police.
   ____
4. People who smoke inside the building may be fined.
   ____
5. Guadeloupe, which is an island territory of France, is located in the Caribbean Sea.
   ____
6. Any student who breaks school rules will be punished.
   ____
7. The file that holds all the documentation of the study was accidentally misplaced.
   ____

WRITING Restrictive and non-restrictive adjective clauses

A **PREWRITING: USING WH–QUESTIONS** Think about an incident in your life that you regret. Then write Wh–questions about the incident to help generate ideas.

Who ______________________________

What ______________________________

When ______________________________

Where ______________________________

Why ______________________________

How ______________________________

Answer your questions on a separate sheet of paper. Read what you wrote and add other ideas.

B **WRITING** On a separate sheet of paper, describe the experience that you regret, using the answers to your questions. Include details, using adjective clauses when possible.

C **SELF-CHECK**

- ☐ Did I include at least three adjective clauses?
- ☐ Did I distinguish between essential and additional information?
- ☐ Did I use commas correctly in non-restrictive adjective clauses?

WRITING MODEL

When I was sixteen years old, I had a part-time job at an ice cream store. I always worked on weekends. If I wanted to make plans to do something with friends, I had to request time off from work in advance.

One week a band that was one of my favorites was coming to town for a concert. My friends and I bought tickets. We couldn't wait! I requested the night off from work weeks ahead of time. I wanted to be sure that the plans were set.

Then, on the day of the concert I got a call from another girl, Shelly, who worked at the store. She was older than me, and she'd worked there longer than I had. She said a guy who she really liked had asked her out that night, but she was supposed to work. She asked me to go in for her. I said I couldn't because I was going to the concert. She'd have to work or figure something else out.

A little while later my boss called. He said that Shelly was really sick and she couldn't work that night. He asked me to go in instead. I couldn't believe it! She was lying to our boss! I told my boss that I had plans and couldn't do it, but he said that he really needed me and that he was counting on me. I caved in. I went in to work that night, and I missed the concert.

That was a decision which I've always regretted.

UNIT 3

Fears, Hardships, and Heroism

PREVIEW

1 Read the quotes.

1. "Do one thing every day that scares you."
—Eleanor Roosevelt

2. "Fear doesn't shut you down; it wakes you up."
—Veronica Roth

3. "Fear is the mind-killer. Fear is the little-death that brings total obliteration."
—Frank Herbert

4. "Fear cuts deeper than swords."
—George R. R. Martin

5. "I'm not afraid of death; I just don't want to be there when it happens."
—Woody Allen

6. "We can easily forgive a child who is afraid of the dark; the real tragedy of life is when men are afraid of the light."
—attributed to Plato

7. "I'm not afraid of storms, for I'm learning how to sail my ship."
—Louisa May Alcott

8. "It is fear, I think, that makes one cling nostalgically to the last moment or clutch greedily toward the next."
—Anne Morrow Lindbergh

Now write what you think each quote means.

1. ______________________________
2. ______________________________
3. ______________________________
4. ______________________________
5. ______________________________
6. ______________________________
7. ______________________________
8. ______________________________

2 **Pick one of the quotes from Exercise 1 and write about what it means to you. How does it apply to your life and how you approach your fears?**

____

____

____

____

____

3 **Complete the conversations with expressions from the box.**

a big deal	it's not the end of the world	take the plunge
be in hot water	jump to that conclusion	with all my heart
freak me out	just chill	you look like you've lost your best friend
got cold feet	mark my words	
have a minor case of the jitters	pulled the rug out from under	

1. A: What's wrong? ______________.
   B: Oh, I just have a lot on my mind.
2. A: Uh-oh. I just broke Mom's tablet.
   B: Uh-oh is right. You're going to ______________.
3. A: Hi Jane. How did the dance competition go?
   B: I didn't end up competing. I ______________.
4. A: Wow, my boss really ______________ me today.
   B: What happened?
5. A: She had promised me a raise, but today she said she couldn't give it to me until next year.
   B: Are you going to look for another job, or ______________ until next year?
6. A: What's your dream in life?
   B: I want to be an astronaut. It'll be a lot of work, but I want it ______________.
7. A: Did you buy that car you were looking at?
   B: No, I didn't end up getting it after all. I just couldn't ______________.
8. A: Lars said he'd call me last night, but I never heard from him. He must not be interested.
   B: I wouldn't ______________.
9. A: Jenny looked really nervous before her job interview.
   B: I know. I can see why. This interview is ______________ for her.
10. A: Yikes!
    B: That? It's just a little spider.
    A: I know, but spiders ______________.

11. **A:** Have you heard from that university in California yet?
    B: Yes. I didn't get in.
    A: Well, ______________________. You'll get into another school.

12. B: I hope so.
    A: ______________________. You will.

13. **A:** What's wrong? You look nervous.
    B: I am. I have a big presentation this morning. I ______________________.

> **Did you know . . .** that it's possible to literally be scared to death? The actual cause of death is a heart attack brought on by sudden, intense stress. And although there are hundreds of documented cases of people actually dying of fright, the statistics aren't as impressive as they might at first seem. Eighty-five to ninety percent of victims had heart disease, and their already weak hearts were pushed beyond their limits by the emotional jolt of fear.

LESSON 1

4 **Choose the best sentence to complete each conversation.**

1. **A:** That's the third time this week my car has broken down. _____
   B: Looks like it's time for a new car.
   a. I've had it! **b.** Don't give up!

2. **A:** Ooh. I really didn't do well on that test.
   B: _____ You'll do better on the next one.
   a. I know what you mean. **b.** Don't let it get you down.

3. **A:** How did your interview go?
   B: Not well. I really don't think I'm going to get the job.
   A: _____ I bet the next one will go better.
   a. Hang in there. **b.** I know what you mean.

4. **A:** _____ I can't figure out this math problem.
   B: Let me see if I can help.
   a. I give up! **b.** That must be frustrating!

5. **A:** I've been taking tennis lessons for a year, but I'm not getting any better.
   B: ______________
   a. I know what you mean. **b.** That must be discouraging.

5 **Complete the sentences with no matter + who, what, when, why, where, or how.**

1. My grandmother hated to be told she couldn't do something.
   ___No matter who___ tried to discourage her, she never gave up her dream of becoming a pilot.
2. Georgia was really frustrated with the last company she worked for. She put in a lot of long hours, but ______________ hard she worked, her boss never gave her any recognition.
3. That story is completely false. ______________ told it to you, there's no way that there's any truth to it. It's only a rumor.
4. There's never a good time to talk to Harry about that. ______________ I bring up the subject, he never wants to discuss it.
5. ______________ anyone tells her, she's going to do what she wants. She's not taking anyone's advice.
6. Tracy and Jack are still trying to choose a location for their wedding. ______________ they decide to have it, I'm sure everything will be gorgeous. They have such great taste.
7. Credit card companies don't care if you have a good reason for making your payment past the due date. ______________ you're late, they still charge you a fee.

LESSON 2

6 **Complete the statements, using so...(that) or such...(that) and the words in parentheses.**

1. The weather was ______________________ I decided to walk to work. (beautiful)
2. My meal was ______________________ I ate the whole thing and ordered more. (delicious)
3. That was ______________________ my ears are still ringing. (a loud concert)
4. The film was ______________________ I had to leave the movie theater. (scary)
5. She gave ______________________ no one wanted it to end. (a good speech)
6. Ella performed ______________________ she has a chance to be on the Olympic team. (well)
7. Your room is ______________________ you really need to spend the weekend cleaning. (messy)
8. The week went by ______________________ I feel like we just got here. (quickly)
9. Todd made ______________________ it was gone within an hour. (fresh lemonade)

7 **Complete each statement with so + much, little, many, or few.**

1. ____________ people signed up for the class that they had to cancel it.
2. There were ____________ cars in the parking lot that I couldn't find a place to park.
3. There were ____________ storms in the area that our plane had to land in another city.
4. We had ____________ time in Montreal that we really didn't get to see much of the city.
5. There are ____________ forms to fill out that I'm not sure I'll finish in time.
6. ____________ children came to the party that the room was almost empty.
7. I ate ____________ lunch that I wasn't hungry for dinner.

8 **CHALLENGE Rewrite each sentence, using such...(that).**

1. The concert was so good that I didn't want to leave.

   It was *such a good concert that I didn't want to leave*.
2. That blouse is so pretty that I think I'll buy it.

   It's ____________.
3. This day was so frustrating that I'm glad it's almost over.

   This was ____________.
4. Stu's voicemail was so encouraging that I feel much better.

   Stu left ____________.
5. The weather was so bad that we canceled the party.

   It was ____________.

9 **Answer the questions.**

1. People react to fearful situations differently. What physical symptoms are most likely when you are afraid? ____________
2. What type of situation might cause you to get butterflies in your stomach? ____________

   ____
3. Movies and television programs often show frightening events. Why do you think people want to watch things that scare them? ____________

   ____

10 **Read the true story about confronting adversity. Then answer the questions.**

Gender
Female
Male

Age
Under 20
20-40
40-60
60-80
80-100

Location
Africa
Asia
Australia
Europe
North America
South America

STORIES THAT INSPIRE Sign In | Home |

Terry Fox: The Marathon of Hope

In 1977 Terry Fox was an athletic teenager growing up near Vancouver, British Columbia. But X-rays taken after Fox felt sharp pains in his right knee revealed unthinkable results: bone cancer. Fox's right leg was amputated 15 centimeters above the knee when he was only eighteen.

But Fox wouldn't be discouraged. Just three weeks after his surgery, he was walking with an artificial leg. He took up sports and running again, and then fostered a new, incredible plan: to run across Canada and raise money for cancer research. He set a goal of $1 for every Canadian. In letters he sent asking for sponsorship, he said: "I'm not saying that this will initiate any kind of definitive answer or cure to cancer, but I believe in miracles. I have to." He called his run "The Marathon of Hope."

On April 12, 1980, Fox splashed his artificial leg in the Atlantic Ocean and began his coast-to-coast run. He ran 42 kilometers a day (the equivalent of a marathon!) through the provinces of Newfoundland, Quebec, and Ontario. News of Fox's journey and the money he collected grew. By the time he reached Toronto, he had attained celebrity status. Crowds lined the streets to watch him pass by, providing a flood of emotional and financial support.

But on September 1, after 143 days, adversity rose again. Cancer had appeared in Fox's lungs, forcing him to stop running. At a press conference announcing the news, he said, "I just wish people would realize that anything's possible if you try. Dreams are made if people try." Inspired by these words, people rallied to collect even more money. By February 1981, $24.17 million had been raised, equal to Canada's population at the time. But while Fox's dream was coming true, he was fighting for his life. The cancer progressed quickly. Canada and the world were devastated when Terry Fox passed away on June 28, 1981, at age 22.

That September, the first Terry Fox Run was held. Over 300,000 people participated, raising $3.5 million. Terry Fox Runs are now held in 60 countries annually, through which more than $360 million has been raised for cancer research.

1. What obstacles did Terry Fox face? Which did he overcome? ______________________

____

2. How would you describe Fox's attitude in dealing with adversity? If you were faced with challenges like Fox's, what do you think your attitude would be? ______________________

____

3. Do you know someone who has inspired people by overcoming an obstacle? What obstacle did the person overcome? ______________________

____

11 **CHALLENGE** **Reread the article about Marlee Matlin on page 32 in the Student's Book. Compare Marlee Matlin and Terry Fox. How are they similar? How are they different? Complete the diagram to compare these two people.**

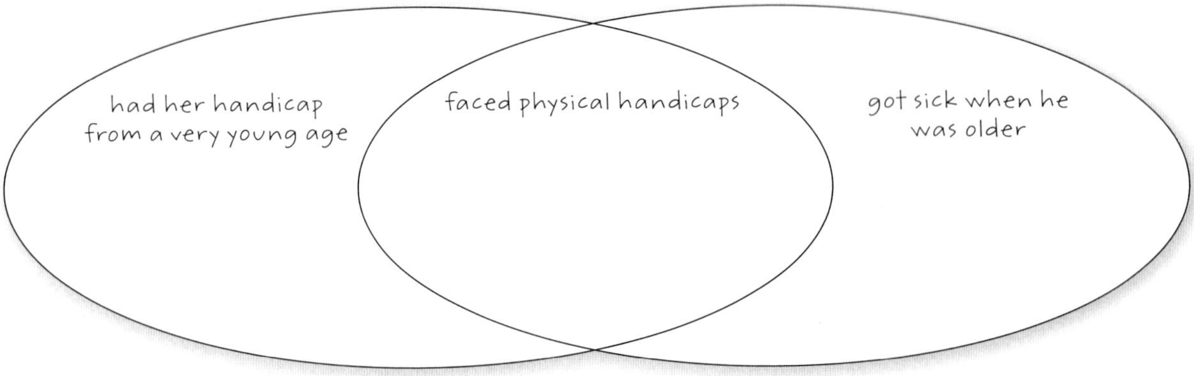

Marlee Matlin **Both** **Terry Fox**

LESSON 4

12 **Complete the chart with the correct parts of speech.**

Adjective	Adverb	Noun
brave	bravely	bravery
willing		
courageous		
	heroically	
	fearlessly	
		confidence

13 **Complete the sentences. Use words from the chart in Exercise 12. There may be more than one correct answer.**

1. Although Jim has studied French for many years, he lacks ________________ in his language ability. He never speaks in class because he's sure that he'll make a lot of mistakes.
2. Tessa ________________ jumped in the water to save the little girl who couldn't swim.
3. My neighbor helped a lot of people escape from their houses after the flood. The mayor gave her a medal for her ________________ actions.
4. The salespeople at the All-Terrain Sports Shop are always ________________ to help their customers. They usually offer to help before you even ask.
5. When the firefighter heard that several children were trapped in their bedrooms, he repeatedly entered the burning house to rescue them. The firefighter was honored for his ________________.
6. My two-year-old son isn't afraid of anything—he loves climbing, jumping, and swimming. He even loves snakes and spiders! He's completely ________________.

14 **Read the profile of Paul Rusesabagina. Then answer the questions.**

The Courage and Compassion of an Ordinary Man

Paul Rusesabagina, a manager of the Hotel Mille Collines in the Rwandan capital of Kigali, did not consider himself an extraordinary man. He was, however, an exceptionally effective businessman, skilled at using his connections with the rich and powerful to keep his hotel running smoothly and to obtain the best of everything for his hotel guests. He knew, for example, that flattering words and gifts of imported liquor and cigars would win him favors from government officials.

Paul Rusesabagina saved the lives of over 1,200 people during the Rwandan genocide of 1994.

But on April 6, 1994, neither Rusesabagina nor most Rwandans could get the only thing that they wanted: safety. On that day, an ethnic group known as the Hutus began killing another ethnic group, the Tutsis. As a Hutu, Rusesabagina was safe. But his wife, a Tutsi, and their three children, were not. With his thoughts focused on his family, Rusesabagina took them to the hotel for safety. He didn't consider taking in other Tutsis or making the hotel a refuge. But as people arrived at the hotel begging for help, he felt he had no choice. Rusesabagina ended up accepting over 1,200 refugees into the hotel.

For 100 days while the killing went on outside, Rusesabagina held off the soldiers from invading the hotel. He used money and luxury goods from the hotel to bribe them. He called in every favor owed to him. When the killing was finally over, Rusesabagina, his family, and most of the refugees had survived.

1. Why do you think Paul Rusesabagina did not consider himself an extraordinary man?

____

____

2. According to the profile, what special talents or abilities did Rusesabagina have?

____

____

3. Do you think that Rusesabagina's experiences or actions in Rwanda made him a hero? Explain why or why not.

____

____

GRAMMAR BOOSTER

A **Combine the two parts of each item to write an embedded question.**

1. Why is Jane afraid to fly? (I wonder)

 ____

2. When will our guests arrive? (Do you know)

 ____

3. Where is the office? (Can you tell me)

 ____

4. How far is it to San Francisco? (Would you mind telling me)

 ____

5. How did the pilot land the plane safely in the water? (I don't know)

 ____

6. Is Mary disappointed that she didn't get the job? (Do you think)

 ____

7. Can we stay after class? (Let's ask)

 ____

8. How many people were at the event? (I'd like to know)

 ____

9. Did I turn off the stove? (I can't remember)

 ____

10. Would Dana like to come with us? (Let's ask)

 ____

B **Complete each sentence. Circle the correct word.**

1. A **cloud** / **clap** / **gust** of smoke covered the burning building.
2. There's a **can** / **box** / **tube** of detergent for the dishwasher under the sink.
3. Would you mind picking up a **loaf** / **carton** / **liter** of bread for dinner?
4. A **clap** / **bolt** / **ray** of sunshine cut through the cloudy sky.
5. I'd like a **liter** / **cup** / **glass** of coffee with cream and sugar, please.
6. The recipe calls for one **drop** / **clove** / **bar** of garlic.
7. A **drop** / **bar** / **gust** of wind lifted the kite into the sky.

C **Complete each sentence with a phrase from the box. Each phrase will be used more than once.**

an act of	a piece of	a sense of	a state of

1. Let me give you ________________ advice.
2. After the changes were implemented, many of the employees were in ________________ confusion.
3. Mrs. Carson always maintains ________________ control in her classroom.
4. The students' refusal to attend classes was ________________ defiance.
5. After finally finishing the project, we enjoyed ________________ accomplishment.
6. To do this job, it's really helpful to have ________________ humor.
7. That's just ________________ gossip. I wouldn't pay any attention to it.
8. After standing empty for over 20 years, the old house was in ________________ disrepair.

D **Choose the correct noun to complete each sentence.**

1. There's _____ it will rain tomorrow.
   a. a chance　　b. chance
2. Do you like _____?
   a. a fruit　　b. fruit
3. I've planned everything—I'm not leaving anything to _____.
   a. a chance　　b. chance
4. Did you use _____ on your hair?
   a. a shampoo　　b. shampoo
5. There's _____ on the table. Can you turn it on, please?
   a. a light　　b. light
6. Gold is _____ that is fairly soft.
   a. a metal　　b. metal
7. There's so much _____ coming through the windows.
   a. a light　　b. light

WRITING Reducing adverbial clauses

A **PREWRITING: "FREEWRITING" FOR IDEAS**

- Choose a story about a hero. It can be a true or fictional story. It could be about someone you know personally or someone famous. On a separate sheet of paper, write for five to ten minutes all the details about the story you can think of. Write quickly. Do not take time to correct spelling, punctuation, verb forms, time order, etc.
- Then read what you wrote. Choose ideas you would like to develop and put them in logical order.

B **WRITING** On a separate sheet of paper, tell your story. Use adverbial clauses and phrases as well as prepositional time phrases and sequencing words and phrases to narrate past events logically. Use the story about Paul Rusesabagina in Exercise 14 as a model.

C **SELF-CHECK**

☐ Did I write two or more paragraphs?

☐ Does my report tell the story in the order that the events occurred?

☐ Did I use at least three adverbial clauses or reduced adverbial phrases to clarify time relationships?

Prepositional time phrases
on Fridays
in May
from January to May
at 8:00
by April
during that time

Sequencing words and phrases
First,
Next,
Then,
After that,
Finally

UNIT

4 Getting Along with Others

PREVIEW

1 Read the website.

Sign In | Home |

A Better You

If you're like most people, then there are probably a few things you'd like to change or improve in your life. Check out this list of the most common resolutions that people make. Notice any of yours among them? Click on any that sound familiar for links that'll help you follow through with your good intentions.

Physical Health
Eating
Exercise
Nutrition
Vitamins

Mental Health
Meditation
Stress Reduction
Support Groups
Therapy

- **Spend more time with loved ones.**
  What fun is life if you don't share it with the people you care about most? If you don't have enough time for them, then you've got to make time. They'll appreciate it, and you'll reap the benefits, too.
- **Get in shape.**
  You'll look and feel better if you start taking care of your body. The health benefits of regular exercise are substantial, and maintaining a healthy weight is vital to reducing the risk of illness and increasing longevity.
- **Help others.**
  Whether it's teaching a child to read, volunteering in your community, or building a house, there are so many ways to make a difference in someone's life. Charitable organizations always welcome donations of time, money, and talent.
- **Manage your money.**
  Is money a big source of stress in your life? Whether you want to get out of debt, increase your savings, or just start spending more sensibly, there are lots of ways to get a handle on your finances.
- **Manage your time.**
  Not enough hours in a day to get everything done that you need to? That may be true, but you can still accomplish a lot by simply prioritizing your activities and carefully planning when and how often to do each one.
- **Break a habit.**
  Whether it's smoking, drinking too much coffee, or spending beyond your means, many of us have habits that are self-destructive. Willpower is the key to fighting habits that bring us temporary pleasure but can cause harm in the long run.

Now read the interviews. For each person, choose the resolution on the website that best matches the person's goal or situation.

1. "My goal? That's easy. I want to fit into the suit I wore when I got married. I tried the suit on last week, and I couldn't even button the vest. I've only been married a year and a half! I think every guy thinks he's just a few sit-ups away from a flat, washboard stomach. It was a shock to see how much weight I've gained in such a short time."
   —Jared Strong, Calgary, Canada

   ____

2. "I'm really fortunate that I had the opportunity to receive a good education. I know that there are lots of kids who weren't as lucky as I was, and I'd like to do something to give them a chance to learn. Maybe I could volunteer at a local school as a reading or math coach."
   —Amala Singh, Mumbai, India

   ____

3. "I spent my twenties focused on getting the next big promotion, more responsibility at my job, and a higher salary. Now I look back and realize that my job was my whole life. From now on I want to spend more evenings and weekends with my family and start accepting my friends' invitations to get together."
   —Christobal Valenzuela de Barros, Lima, Peru

   ____

4. "I make a decent salary, but I just can't save up enough money to buy my own home. Everything I earn gets spent on clothes, nice restaurant meals, and movies. I wonder if I'm handling my finances as wisely as I could."
   —Fumiyo Ikeda, Nagoya, Japan

   ____

2 **WHAT ABOUT YOU? Answer the questions.**

1. Do you think any of the resolutions on the website might be helpful to you? Why or why not?

   ____

   ____

   ____

2. Do you ever make resolutions about things in your life that you'd like to change or improve? If so, have you been successful in following through with these goals?

   ____

   ____

   ____

3 **Read the situations. Then identify the shortcoming that each person needs to overcome.**

a perfectionist	controlling	hot-tempered	oversensitive
a procrastinator	disorganized	negative	

1. Tanya spends more time looking for all the things she'll need to do a project than she spends working on the project itself. Nothing is where she thinks she left it or where it should be. She's ____________.
2. With the due date for a big assignment quickly approaching, Trevor just can't seem to make himself do it. He'll do anything to avoid it, even clean the house, do the laundry, or go to the gym—activities that he normally hates. Trevor is ____________.
3. You can't criticize Pam at all. She gets hurt or angry if you say even the smallest negative thing to her. Even if you're not criticizing her, she takes it the wrong way. Pam is ____________.
4. It's not fun to be in the car when Loren is driving. He gets angry at the other drivers over the smallest things. If someone drives too slowly, or turns without signaling, he gets red in the face and starts yelling. It's annoying. Loren is ____________.
5. Bruce seems to have a hard time focusing on what's good about a situation. He tends to see the bad things about it, or all of the things that could go wrong. Bruce is ____________.
6. Janet needs to be in charge of everything. She can't let her employees make decisions for themselves, even about small things. Janet is ____________.
7. David never seems to be happy with his artwork. He's a great painter, but he always sees how he could have made each painting better. David is ____________.

4 **WHAT ABOUT YOU? Answer the questions.**

1. Describe a time when you (or someone you know) lost your cool.

____

____

2. What kinds of things can set you off?

____

____

3. Have you ever told anyone off? Has anyone ever told you off? Explain.

____

____

4. Have you ever had to walk on eggshells around someone? Explain.

____

____

5. Has anyone ever taken something out on you unfairly? Explain.

____

____

LESSON 1

5 **Write sentences using <u>even if</u> or <u>whether or not</u> and a clause from column 1, combined with a clause from column 2.**

1. we had set an alarm	she still tends to feel hurt
2. you don't mean to criticize Ellen	my room still ends up being a mess
3. you tell Daniel his work is excellent	we still would have missed the bus
4. it's not a big deal	my boss will still make a big issue out of it
5. I try to be organized	he will probably tell you how he'd like to improve it
6. I had brought the issue up privately	Jen would probably still have overreacted

1. *Even if we had set an alarm, we still would have missed the bus.*
2. ______________________________
3. ______________________________
4. ______________________________
5. ______________________________
6. ______________________________

6 **Complete the sentences, using <u>only if</u>.**

1. *Only if* ______ you get started now *will you* ______ have time to finish the job.
2. Tom will succeed in controlling his temper ______________ works hard at it.
3. ______________ Jennifer gets more organized ______________ get a promotion.
4. Your problem will affect your career ______________ make a big issue out of it.
5. Tony will do well ______________ thinks positively.
6. ______________ I write a note to myself ______________ remember to run that errand.

CHALLENGE **Now rewrite the sentences above, reversing the order of the clauses.**

1. *You will have time to finish the job only if you get started now.*
2. ______________________________
3. ______________________________
4. ______________________________
5. ______________________________
6. ______________________________

7 **Choose the correct word or phrase to complete each sentence.**

1. ______ he apologizes for yelling at me, I won't help him with his project.
   a. Unless b. Only if
2. Can you call me at 6:30 tomorrow morning? ______, I'm afraid I'll sleep in.
   a. Unless b. Otherwise
3. ______ it makes you uncomfortable, I still think you should tell him what's bothering you.
   a. Even if b. Only if
4. We won't make it to the airport on time ______ we leave right now.
   a. unless b. if only
5. Things are going to change, ______ we're ready.
   a. unless b. whether or not
6. Only if you learn to control your temper ______ succeed at this company.
   a. will you b. you will
7. I have to put things away as soon as I'm finished using them. ______, I forget where I left them.
   a. Whether or not b. Otherwise
8. ______ Jack loses his temper easily, he usually calms down pretty quickly.
   a. Even if b. Only if

LESSON 2

8 **Rewrite each sentence as a cleft sentence with What. Use the correct from of be.**

1. I don't understand procrastination.
   What I don't understand is procrastination.
2. I love getting surprised with flowers.
   ____
3. You need a day off.
   ____
4. The dozens of people who visited Eileen at the hospital made her happy.
   ____
5. Seeing so many people at the reception made me grateful.
   ____
6. I didn't expect the many rules and regulations here.
   ____

9 **Combine each pair of sentences by writing a cleft sentence with What and a noun clause subject complement.**

1. You were late for the presentation. It bothered me.
   What bothered me was that you were late for the presentation.
2. James is so sensitive. It surprises me.
   ____
3. You need to be more organized. That's what she means.
   ____
4. I really appreciated your help yesterday. That's what I was trying to say.
   ____
5. We didn't know anyone at the party. It made us uncomfortable.
   ____
6. You need to be more easygoing. That's what I think.
   ____

10 **Rewrite each sentence as a cleft sentence with It.**

1. Max made us late.
   It was Max who made us late.
2. Yuki's perfectionism annoys me.
   ____
3. The fact that you forgot your anniversary made her angry.
   ____
4. Karl's negativity bothers his co-workers.
   ____
5. Good friends make all the difference.
   ____
6. The final exam is the most important.
   ____

LESSON 3

11 **Read about the people. Then summarize the way each person handles anger. Use expressions from the box. There may be more than one correct answer.**

blow one's top	keep it inside	lose one's temper
calm down	let it go	shrug it off
hold it in	let off steam	vent

Because Joe works as a salesperson, he has to be nice to customers all the time, even if they really make him angry. When he gets home after a bad day at work, he sometimes needs to talk to his wife about it. That helps.

Beth found an effective way to control her anger. Whenever she gets mad, she leaves the office and takes a 10-minute walk. When she gets back to the office, she's usually in a much better mood and she's better able to deal with her problem.

After several weeks of being badly treated by his boss, Luis finally got ticked off and yelled at him. Surprisingly, his boss didn't fire him. He actually gave Luis a few days off and began treating him better.

Maggie had a bad day at work today. Several of her clients were rude and yelled at her. But Maggie's pretty easygoing. She just said, "They can get mad if they want to. I'm not going to let it bother me."

1. (Joe) ______________________
2. (Beth) ______________________
3. (Luis) ______________________
4. (Maggie) ______________________

12 **Read the story.**

There once was a woman who always bought fruit and vegetables from the same local farmer. This farmer had earned a good reputation for the freshness and tastiness of his produce, which he delivered himself in an old truck.

Then, one day, the woman planned a large dinner party. She placed a large order with the farmer to be delivered on the day of the party. However, the day of the party arrived and the farmer did not deliver the goods as promised. Without the necessary ingredients, the woman was unable to cook the wonderful meal that her guests expected. Short of food, she was embarrassed that many of her guests left her party hungry.

The next morning, the farmer appeared at the door carrying the produce that he had promised. The woman, unable to control her anger, yelled at the man, calling him irresponsible and lazy. She threatened to stop buying his products. "What do you have to say for yourself?" the woman demanded.

The farmer answered,"I'm sorry to have inconvenienced you. I didn't make your delivery yesterday because my mother passed away."

Ashamed about the way she had spoken to the man, the woman vowed never to speak in anger again.

Now summarize the lesson that the woman in the story learned about handling anger. Use the Vocabulary from Student's Book page 44 or your own words.

____

____

____

____

13 **WHAT ABOUT YOU? Complete the sentences in your own way.**

1. When I get ticked off, sometimes I ______________________________.
2. Sometimes I ______________________________ to let off steam.
3. I sometimes lose my temper when ______________________________.
4. When I need to vent I sometimes ______________________________.

LESSON 4

14 **Read the blog post about friendship.**

Comment Share

Getting Along Posted: July 20, 2016

Being There

Just the other day, someone I know in another city posted this on a social networking site: "My paint tray just fell off the ladder. I'm done. I'm just done. I hate everything and I just can't handle moving into this new apartment all by myself." I felt sorry for her, alone in her apartment, with paint all over the place. I could see why it set her off. I commented, "I'm sorry Sara. I know how you must feel." Dozens of other people commented, too. One said, "RATS! I hate when that happens." Another said, "Sorry, Sara. But don't hold on to your negative feelings. Let it go." Maria, who is Sara's neighbor, commented, "I'm coming over NOW!"

Soon after, Maria came over to Sara's place, and let her vent. (Sara talked and yelled for half an hour about how hard things were.) Maria helped her clean up the paint and then finished painting the hallway. Of course, with all that help, Sara was able to calm down.

Sara's experience got me thinking about friendship and social networking. Can a virtual friend be a real friend? This is what I decided. Even if you have a thousand "friends" on a social networking site, it's likely you will have only a few real friends in your life. Here's why.

Can a virtual friend help you clean up the spill?

When something goes wrong in your life, lots of people will sympathize with you and try to make you feel better. Social networking does that very well, and it can be a good thing. Unless you have a friend nearby, though, you probably won't have someone to help you fix things, whether you make a little slip or mess up big time. What I mean is that actually being there to help you pick up the pieces matters. For one thing, friendships are built while we help each other. When someone helps you clean up spilled paint or fix your broken bike, they are showing that you can depend on them. When someone comes to your grandfather's funeral and sits beside you, you are learning that this person truly cares. A virtual friend can cheer you up or give you good advice, but it is the friend who stands next to you who earns your trust.

Can a virtual friend really believe in you?

Most of us have goals in life. Whether or not you are sure you are going to succeed, a friend's belief in you will put the wind beneath your wings. You may post a video of yourself singing online and get a hundred "likes." But when the person shows up at your recital and gives you a vote of confidence in person, you can really feel it. And when someone helps you find new songs, goes shopping with you to look for a recital outfit, and helps you let off steam when you're frustrated, you have a real friend.

Can a virtual friend really know you?

The American writer and historian Henry Adams said, "One friend in a lifetime is much; two are many; three are hardly possible." What Adams is talking about is a very special kind of friend, one who actually knows you. On a social networking site, you choose how you present yourself. What your virtual friends learn about you is entirely up to you. It's not at all the complete picture. But someone who is actually part of your life sees the sorrow even when you try to hold it in and the courage you're too modest to brag about. They also know that you are sometimes too critical and you lose your cool about things that shouldn't really bother you. They know you're not perfect. And they care about you anyway. Only someone who genuinely knows all the parts of you—good and bad—can really accept you as you. That person knows the real you and is, therefore, a true friend. And virtual friends just can't do that.

Now answer the questions.

1. Summarize how the writer defines a "real" friend.

____

____

2. According to the writer, what are some things real friends do that virtual friends cannot do?

____

____

3. What does the writer mean when she says that a real friend "earns your trust"?

____

____

4. Why does the writer feel that online friends can't know the real you?

____

____

15 **WHAT ABOUT YOU? Answer the questions.**

1. Do you agree with the writer's description of what a friend is? Would you define friendship any differently? How?

____

____

2. Do you agree that virtual friends cannot be as "real" or as "good" as friends who are part of your daily life? Explain.

____

____

3. Think about your virtual friends and the friends who are part of your daily life. Do you have any examples to support or refute the writer's opinion? Explain.

____

____

16 **Describe one of your friends. What are this person's strengths? In what ways do you rely on this friend? In what ways does your friend rely on you? Which of the qualities of friendship from Student's Book page 46 apply to your friendship?**

____

____

____

____

____

____

GRAMMAR BOOSTER

A **Complete the sentences. Circle the correct word or phrase.**

1. **Although / As long as / Besides** she drank coffee for over 20 years, my mother has recently switched to green tea.
2. The amount of trash produced in this country has dropped. **Otherwise / Still / In fact**, there are people who throw away things like glass, paper, and aluminum that could be recycled.
3. In my opinion, the high price of those concert tickets is worth it. **That is / Now that / Similarly,** I'd pay $100 to go if tickets were still available.
4. The best ways to lose weight are through a nutritious diet and exercise. **Nonetheless / Whereas / Unless** you change your eating and exercise habits, you'll never get results.
5. Donald Frank is an excellent candidate for the job because of his education. **While / Moreover / As a result,** he has professional experience in the field.
6. Georgia King is very generous with her time. **For instance / Consequently / Furthermore,** last week she volunteered 30 hours at the public library.

B **Complete each sentence with a conjunction or transition from the box.**

as long as	in other words	nonetheless	so
besides	likewise	now that	whether

1. Charlie did poorly at school but was successful in life. ________________, his son James was never a good student but started a very profitable business.
2. ________________ we're tested on this information or not, we should still study it. It could be very useful later on.
3. Bob Alderson really dislikes public speaking. ________________, he does it frequently for his job.
4. People were stressed out for a while. ________________ a decision has been made, everyone is feeling relieved.
5. Clark College appeals to a lot of non-traditional students. ____________ night and weekend classes, the school offers several online courses, which allows people to continue to work while they study.
6. ________________ Jean Hicks continues at her current pace, she'll easily win the race.
7. Lauren Cook has the best sales record in the company. ________________, she's the company's most valuable salesperson.
8. The department head wanted to show his appreciation for the employees' efforts, ________________ he took the entire group out to lunch.

C **Combine each pair of sentences into one sentence. Use the conjunction or transition in parentheses and the correct punctuation.**

1. Harry has only studied Italian for a year. He is the best student in the class. (however)

   Harry has only studied Italian for a year; however, he is the best student in the class.
2. Karen has a good head for numbers. She's very good at chemistry and physics. (furthermore)

   ____

3. We're facing a big challenge. We're managing to stay positive. (even though)

____

4. Sharon is saving money right now. She can buy a house in a few years. (so that)

____

5. I don't really like vegetables. I eat them because they're good for me. (though)

____

6. Lucia disliked the ring that her husband gave her on their anniversary. She wore it every day to avoid hurting his feelings. (yet)

____

D **Complete the answers with information about yourself and your friends. Complete each answer with a cleft sentence with What, using the underlined information.**

1. Are you looking forward to relaxing this weekend?

   Actually, *what I'm looking forward to is going to the gym.*

2. Do your friends like going to concerts?

   Actually, ______________________________

3. Does it bother you when someone interrupts you?

   Actually, ______________________________

4. Would your friends say that you're oversensitive?

   Actually, ______________________________

5. Do you enjoy exercising?

   Actually, ______________________________

6. Are you looking forward to spending time with your family this weekend?

   Actually, ______________________________

E **Restate the answers, using cleft sentences with It to clarify who, what, when, where, or why.**

1. **A:** Did they decide to have the meeting in Boston?

   B: (They decided to have it in Houston.) Actually, *it was Houston where they decided to have it*.

2. **A:** Did you yell at your boss in the meeting today?

   B: (I didn't, but Janie did.) Actually, ______________________________.

3. **A:** Do long meetings really bother Gretchen?

   B: (They don't, but unnecessary meetings do.) No. It's ______________________________.

4. **A:** Is the restaurant usually crowded at 6:00?

   B: (No, but it's crowded from 7 to 8:30.) No, usually ______________________________.

5. **A:** Are you mad because Tammy interrupted you?

   B: (I'm mad because she's always late.) No, ______________________________.

"Don't ask yourself what the world needs—ask yourself what makes you come alive, and then go do that. Because what the world needs is people who have come alive."

—Harold Thurman Whitman, philosopher and theologian

WRITING Transitional topic sentences

A **PREWRITING: OUTLINING** You are going to write some tips for making a change. Choose one of the changes in the box or think of your own. Write it on the line labeled "Change" and then propose three ways of making the change.

Change: ______________________________

Ways to make the change:

1. ______________________________
2. ______________________________
3. ______________________________

Changes:
- Overcome a shortcoming
- Reduce stress
- Manage anger
- Adopt a new lifestyle
- Your own idea:

____

Example:

Change: *overcome perfectionism*

Ways to make the change:

1. *be less critical of myself when I make mistakes*
2. *learn to accept myself the way I am*
3. *set realistic goals*

B **WRITING** On a separate piece of paper, develop each way listed in Exercise A into a paragraph. Start all three paragraphs with topic sentences. Be sure to use a transitional topic sentence for paragraphs 2 and 3.

Presenting contrasting information
Although
However,
On the other hand, . . .
Even though . . .
Despite the fact that . . .
Nevertheless, . . .

C **SELF-CHECK**

- ☐ Does the first paragraph have a topic sentence?
- ☐ Do the paragraphs that follow have transitional topic sentences?
- ☐ Does each transitional topic sentence clearly link to previous content?

Presenting additional information
Furthermore, . . .
Moreover, . . .
More importantly,

UNIT 5

Humor

PREVIEW

1 Look at the photos.

A

B

C

D

Do you find any of the photos funny? Why or why not?

____

____

2 Answer the questions.

1. Have you ever tried to say something funny, only to have it go over like a lead balloon? Explain.
____
2. Describe a time when you (or someone you know) made a total fool of yourself. ______________
____
3. What is something that just isn't done in your culture? Why? ______________
____
4. What is something people do that you just don't get? ______________
____
5. What is a piece of advice you've been given that is easier said than done? ______________
____

3 **Answer the questions. Then read the article.**

1. Do you believe that you laugh more or less than most people? Do you believe that there are health benefits to laughter?

   ____

2. What could people do to spend more time laughing? ______________________________

   ____

Laughter Clubs Make Health a Laughing Matter

Dr. Madan Kataria, founder of laughter yoga

Nowadays most doctors agree that laughter provides a number of health benefits. But the challenge is to get people to start laughing.

In 1995, Dr. Madan Kataria, a physician from Mumbai, India, came up with a solution: laughter clubs. He has said that the idea for a laughter club came to him "like a divine light." People join groups for all sorts of motivation, learning, and support. Why not to laugh?

In the first few laughter club meetings, group members took turns telling jokes. But after a few weeks people had a hard time finding new jokes. Some started telling dirty and offensive jokes. So Dr. Kataria revised his idea. He decided that the club members needed to learn to laugh without any jokes or source of humor.

Dr. Kataria developed a method of self-induced laughter, which he called laughter yoga. Explaining a little about the method, he said, "In a nutshell, laughter yoga is a combination of self-induced laughter, yoga exercises, yoga breathing, and stretching exercises."

He advised, "Start with a large group—the bigger, the better." Each laughter club gathering starts with a deep-breathing exercise, followed by chanting the syllables ho-ho-ha-ha-ha. Members then participate in laughter exercises, or simulated laughter. An important part of this step is for group members to make eye contact with one another. Dr. Kataria explained, "With a little bit of playfulness it becomes real laughter." And the laughter is contagious.

Most group members said that at first it felt strange to laugh for no reason. But they got used to it, and they like Dr. Kataria's methods. The laughter yoga movement has spread quickly. There are now over 5,000 laughter clubs in 40 countries around the world.

4 **Reread the article in Exercise 3. Circle three examples of direct speech and underline two examples of indirect speech. Then rewrite the sentences with direct speech as indirect speech.**

1. ______________________________
2. ______________________________
3. ______________________________

5 **Rewrite each quotation in indirect speech.**

1. One woman reported, "I've never laughed so hard in my life!"

 ___

2. A laughter yoga teacher advised me, "Let go of your inhibitions."

 ___

3. A man admitted, "I was laughing to the point of crying!"

 ___

4. Before his first session, he thought, "I can't make myself laugh in front of other people."

 ___

5. An experienced member warned me, "You might feel a little uncomfortable at first."

 ___

6. After her first meeting, a woman said, "I'll be here again next week."

 ___

7. Some laughter club members claim, "The group has changed our lives."

 ___

8. One doctor said, "I'm recommending laughter yoga to all my patients."

 ___

9. The doctor insisted, "Laughter is good medicine."

 ___

10. He said, "I would join the health club if it didn't cost so much money."

 ___

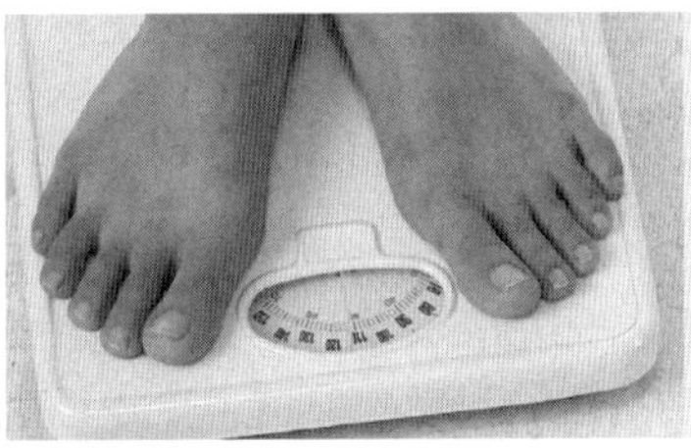

Laughing out loud for 10 to 15 minutes burns between 10 and 40 calories, depending on a person's body weight. This translates to a potential weight loss of approximately 4.5 pounds (approximately 2 kilograms) a year if you do it every day.

6 **Read the conversation in direct speech. Then complete the sentences in indirect speech. Circle the correct words or phrases.**

Buck: Have you heard the weather report?
Henry: It's supposed to be cold tomorrow.
Buck: Well, it'll be like every other day this week then.
Henry: Yeah, I'm tired of the cold weather.
Buck: Me, too. I can't wait for spring.

1. Buck asked if Henry **has heard / had heard** the weather report.
2. Henry said it **was / had been** supposed to be cold **the next day / that day**.
3. Buck replied that it **would be / would have been** like every other day **that week / last week.**
4. Henry said that **I am / he was** tired of the cold weather.
5. Buck agreed and said he **didn't wait / couldn't wait** for spring.

7 Look at the comic strip. Complete the characters' conversation in your own way.

Now rewrite the characters' words as indirect speech.

1. *The boy advised the pirate that there was a storm coming.*
2. ____________________
3. ____________________
4. ____________________
5. ____________________
6. ____________________

LESSON 2

8 Complete the conversation. Circle the correct words.

John: Hey, I have a new joke. Here goes . . . Which animal should you never trust?
Audrey: Um, I don't know.
Natalie: Wait! Don't tell me. Um, . . . OK, I give up.
John: The cheetah!
Natalie: Ha! **That went over my head. / I don't get it. / That's too much!** That joke is hilarious.
Audrey: **That's hysterical. / I don't get it. / That's ridiculous.** Can you explain it?
John: The word "cheetah" sounds like "cheater." You should never trust a cheater.
Audrey: Oh. You know, **that's pretty silly / I don't get it / that's too much.** I mean, it's really not that funny.

People are more likely to laugh when they hear other people laughing. Television producers have capitalized on this fact since the 1950s by adding laugh tracks, or recordings of people laughing, to comedy programs. When we hear others laughing, we actually feel that the show is more humorous.

9 **Rewrite each question in indirect speech.**

1. Ann asked, "Did you think that comedian was funny?"

 ____

2. Sophia asked, "Are you going to the party tonight?"

 ____

3. Tom asked me, "How do you remember all those jokes?"

 ____

4. Maya asked Jake, "How many years have you been working here?"

 ____

5. Steve asked Hanna, "What time are you going swimming tomorrow?"

 ____

10 **Complete the summary of each conversation. Use indirect speech.**

1. **Pete:** Did you hear the joke about the rude parrot?
 Angela: Yes, I heard it, but I didn't think it was funny.
 Pete asked *if Angela had heard the joke about the rude parrot*.
 Angela said *that she had heard it, but she hadn't thought it was funny*.

2. **Mr. Adams:** How will you get to the city tomorrow?
 Mr. Jensen: I'll take the train.
 Mr. Adams asked ______________________________.
 Mr. Jensen said ______________________________.

3. **Sara:** How many children do you have?
 Alex: I have two boys.
 Sara asked ______________________________.
 Alex said ______________________________.

4. **Stu:** How can you laugh at that childish movie?
 Ben: I actually think it's really funny.
 Stu asked ______________________________.
 Ben answered ______________________________.

5. **Maria:** How long have you been taking comedy classes?
 Dan: I've been taking them for two years.
 Maria asked ______________________________.
 Dan said ______________________________.

11 **Think of a cartoon you've seen or a joke you've heard that made you laugh. Describe the cartoon or write the joke in your own words.**

____

____

____

____

____

"If you're too busy to laugh, you're too busy."
—Unknown

LESSON 3

12 Read the article.

What's so funny?

Want to make people laugh? Then you've got to know what's funny. Here are a few tips to keep in mind if your goal is to tickle some funny bones.

Consider your audience.

Your audience, whether it's your kids in your living room or a paying crowd at an auditorium, must be able to connect with any situation you describe in your jokes. If they can't relate to the joke, or if they don't completely understand it, then it's simply not funny to them. People love jokes that, based on their experience, make them say, "That's so true!" If you have to explain a joke to someone, the person might eventually understand it, but he or she probably won't think it's funny.

This is the reason that many jokes don't translate well into another language. They rely on an understanding of a particular culture. You can translate the words but, without an appreciation for the background, many translated jokes aren't very funny.

Use surprise.

There's a reason that people say, "Stop me if you've heard this one" before telling a joke. If your audience already knows (or can guess) the end of a joke before you tell it, then it's not going to make them laugh. People laugh at the end of a joke because they've been told a story and led toward its ending, (unconsciously) thinking about what will happen next or how it will end. When we hear something that wasn't what we were expecting, we find it funny.

Surprise is part of the reason that you want to learn to tell jokes without laughing. If you laugh, then your listeners expect you to say something funny. If you tell a joke without laughing or smiling, then they're more surprised when you get to the funny part.

Check your timing.

Another important part of humor is timing, or delivering the punch line at the best possible moment. It's often useful to pause before telling the last line of a joke. The reason is that this builds tension. The listener knows the end is coming and is waiting for it. When you finally tell the punch line, the listener feels a sense of relief and is more inclined to laugh.

Now reread the article. Choose the best answer to each question.

1. Which of the following is not included in the article?
   a. an explanation of why people laugh
   b. advice on how to tell a joke
   c. an anecdote about a comic experience

2. What should you keep in mind when choosing an audience for your joke?
   a. that the humor of the joke be easy for someone of any culture to understand
   b. that the audience be able to relate to the situation described in your joke
   c. that the audience be able to understand your explanation, in case they don't get the joke

3. Why do people laugh when they hear the punch line of a joke?
   a. because the ending is unexpected
   b. because they can guess the ending before you say it
   c. because you laugh and smile while telling the joke

4. What is one technique to make a punch line funnier?
   a. speak quickly before the audience can guess the ending
   b. pause before the last line, to build suspense
   c. laugh, to indicate that the funny part is coming

13 **Look at the examples of humor. If you can, explain the intended humor of each item in your own words.**

1. Why do elephants have wrinkled feet?
   Because they tie their shoelaces too tight.

   It's funny because the punch line is a surprise. The audience is expecting a scientific explanation, but instead they get the comic image of an elephant wearing shoes.

2. A woman walked up to a little old man rocking in a chair on his porch.

   "I couldn't help noticing how happy you look," she said. "What's your secret for a long happy life?"

   "I smoke three packs of cigarettes a day," he said. "I also drink ten cups of coffee a day, eat fatty foods, and never exercise."

   "That's amazing," the woman said. "How old are you?"

   "Twenty-six," he said.

   ____

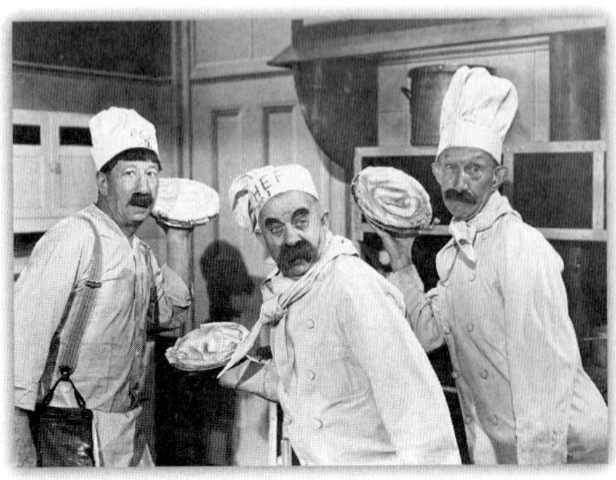

3. ____________________

4. ______________________

____

____

____

Many comedians warn against analyzing humor too much. As American author, poet, and humorist E. B. White once said, "Analyzing humor is like dissecting a frog. Few people are interested and the frog dies of it."

LESSON 4

14 **Do you think it's ever okay to tell the following types of jokes? Why or why not?**

1. a dirty joke ______________________
2. an ethnic joke ______________________
3. a sexist joke ______________________

15 **Read about the practical jokes. Write a sentence about each one. Use the phrases in the box or your own words. There may be more than one correct answer.**

be a good sport	be the butt of a joke	cross the line
be in poor taste	can take a joke	play a joke on someone

Matt asked his friend Adam to help him play a practical joke on Tricia, one of his co-workers. One day, as Matt and Tricia were waiting for their bus after work, Matt asked Tricia to keep an eye on his briefcase for a minute while he ran to a nearby newsstand to buy the paper. Then Adam came running by and "stole" the briefcase. When Matt returned, Tricia explained that someone had stolen the briefcase while she was supposedly watching it. Matt acted really angry and told Tricia that the briefcase contained something very valuable which he thought she should be responsible for replacing. Tricia refused to pay for anything.

A few minutes later, Adam returned with the briefcase and the guys explained the joke. Tricia was angry that Adam frightened her and didn't speak to Matt for a week.

1. *Adam and Matt played a joke on Tricia.*

Jane called a local pizza delivery place and ordered four large pizzas. She gave the name and address of her friend Mark. When the pizza was delivered to Mark's house, Mark was, of course, surprised and confused. The pizza delivery guy insisted that Mark pay for the pizzas. Finally Mark agreed, but he wasn't happy about it.

The next day Jane called her friend and admitted to sending the pizzas. Mark didn't think the joke was very funny since he'd had to pay for food that he didn't want.

2. ______________________________

Jack glued a coin to the sidewalk near the steps of his apartment. He sat down and watched people walking by stop to try to pick it up. When they realized that the coin was glued down, most people looked around to see if anyone was watching, and they looked a little embarrassed.

3. ______________________________

Sue chose a phone number at random out of a telephone book. Through the course of an evening she called the number every half hour and asked to speak with Brian Carr, using a different voice for each call. Each time the woman who answered the phone insisted that Sue had the wrong phone number. After several calls, the woman began to get really annoyed. A few hours later, Sue's friend Bill called the same number. He explained to the woman that his name was Brian Carr and asked if there were any messages for him.

When the woman realized the calls had been a joke, she couldn't help laughing.

4. ______________________________

Did you find any of these practical jokes funny? Why or why not?

____

____

____

16 **WHAT ABOUT YOU?** **Read the quotations. Choose one and summarize its meaning in your own words. Do you agree with the point of view expressed? Explain your answer.**

"It is the ability
to take a joke, not make one,
that proves you have a sense of humor."
—Max Eastman
(American journalist and author)

"Life does not stop
being funny when someone dies, any more
than it stops being serious when someone laughs."
—George Bernard Shaw
(Irish dramatist and literary critic)

"Humor is a rubber sword
— it allows you to make a point
without drawing blood."
—Mary Hirsh
(American humorist, author, teacher)

"The human race has one really
effective weapon, and that is laughter."
—Mark Twain
(American author and humorist)

____

____

____

17 **WHAT ABOUT YOU?** **In your opinion, when does a joke cross the line? Write a short paragraph. Consider some of the ideas below, or use your own. Give at least one example to explain your opinion.**

- if it is intended to make someone feel bad
- if it causes damage to personal property
- if the person who is the butt of the joke doesn't laugh
- if it embarrasses someone
- if it offends someone
- if someone gets hurt

GRAMMAR BOOSTER

A **Read the short conversations and complete the sentences in indirect speech. Then circle all the nouns, pronouns, and possessives that change from direct speech to indirect speech.**

Stan: Stop me if you've heard the joke.

Will: I'll tell you if I know it.

1. Stan said ___to stop___ him if Will ___had heard___ the joke.
2. Will answered that he ___would tell___ Stan if he ___knew___ it.

Maya: When can I expect to receive the finished report?

Ross: Actually, it's on your desk. I left it there earlier.

3. Maya asked when she ________________ to receive the finished report.
4. Ross replied that it ________________ on her desk. He said he ________________ it there earlier.

Kellie: What are you doing this weekend? Is anything interesting going on?

Chris: I don't know. I haven't heard about anything big.

Kellie: Well, give me a call if you want to do something.

5. Kellie asked Chris what he ________________ that weekend. She asked if anything interesting ________________ on.
6. Chris said he ________________. He told Kellie he ________________ about anything big.
7. Kellie told Chris ________________ her a call if he ________________ to do something.

Angie: Will you be able to meet us for dinner?

Grace: I'm not sure. I'll have to check my schedule. I'll call you later to let you know.

8. Angie asked whether she ________________ to meet them for dinner.
9. Grace replied that she ________________ sure. She said she ________________ to check her schedule. She told Angie that she ________________ her later to let her know.

Paula: Could you please move your plant? It's blocking my view.

Steve: I'll move it as soon as I finish these reports.

10. Paula asked Steve ________________ his plant. She said it ________________ her view.
11. Steve replied that he ________________ it as soon as he ________________ the reports.

B **Rewrite each of the following sentences in indirect speech.**

1. Jackie asked Beth, "When did you see Barbara?"

____

2. Seth asked me, "Can you make it to dinner on Tuesday?"

____

3. The teacher ordered the boy, "Put your books on your desk."

____

4. John promised her, "You won't be disappointed."

____

5. Jen told Ben, "Please come to the party at my house on Friday."

____

6. The patient admitted, "I haven't filled my prescription yet."

____

7. My mom told me, "Don't put too much sugar in my coffee."

____

8. Heather asked her sister, "Do you want to go shopping with me?"

____

9. Steve said, "Don't tell me that joke again."

____

C **Mark grammatically correct sentences with a checkmark. Mark incorrect sentences with an *X*. Then correct the incorrect sentences.**

☐ **1.** Hana told to her friend that she didn't find the movie funny.

☐ **2.** Larry said that slapstick was his favorite type of humor.

☐ **3.** Tori asked to Joe if he wanted to get something to eat.

☐ **4.** My boss said me that I was getting a raise.

☐ **5.** I told him that was the funniest joke I'd ever heard.

☐ **6.** Donna asked what the weather forecast was.

☐ **7.** Yoshiko told that the party would be on Friday.

D **Complete the sentences with reporting verbs from the list on Student's Book page 136. Use as many different reporting verbs as you can.**

1. The CEO _______________ that the company had been sold.
2. The newspaper _______________ that the soccer team had won the championship.
3. My dentist _______________ that I needed to floss every day.
4. Harry _______________ that the show really wasn't that funny.
5. Lori _______________ that the play was the best she had ever seen.
6. Luke _______________ that he would text me every day.
7. Jason _______________ that his sister never had to do any work around the house.
8. Phil _______________ that he hadn't made a mistake.

WRITING Writing dialogue

A **PREWRITING: ORDERING EVENTS** Think about a joke or story that you can tell. You don't have to choose a funny story. It can be something that you've experienced, or it can be something you've heard about, read, or seen in a movie or on television. Write a list of the main events that happened. Then make sure the events are in the correct order.

1. ______________________________
2. ______________________________
3. ______________________________
4. ______________________________
5. ______________________________

B **WRITING** On a separate sheet of paper, write the story, telling what happened and what people said. Use dialogue. Each time you use the direct speech of a new speaker, begin a new paragraph.

C **SELF-CHECK**

- ☐ Did I use direct speech in my story?
- ☐ Did I punctuate direct speech correctly?
- ☐ Did I correctly paragraph the dialogue?